The sites described in this directory, a companion to *Visiting Our Past: America's Historylands,* represent places of significance through more than four centuries of our national saga. The list is selective, for some 13,000 sites scattered across the land immortalize the people and commemorate the events that helped shape the United States—far too many for inclusion in a supplement this size.

Entries have been listed alphabetically by state and, wherever appropriate, cross-referenced to the book. Most of the sites include more than one building or relic. Some are original; others are restorations or modern reconstructions based on research. All are open to the public, though some may close down or curtail off-season activities; many charge admission fees. Most places offer the serious visitor at least an hour or two of historic exploration.

If you plan a special visit to an out-of-the-way site, check to be sure it will be open when you arrive. Write to the address listed with the entry or direct your inquiries to the Chamber of Commerce or Town Clerk of the nearest community.

The maps preceding state entries have been keyed to indicate general site locations. In a few Eastern states, such as Virginia, Kentucky, and Massachusetts, several closely grouped sites have been assigned a single number. The following abbreviations for historic designations have been used extensively:

HD—Historic District

HS—Historic Site

NB—National Battlefield

NBP—National Battlefield Park

NBS—National Battlefield Site

NHL—National Historic Landmark

NHS—National Historic Site

NHP—National Historical Park

NMem—National Memorial

NMP—National Military Park

NM—National Monument

NP—National Park

SHL—State Historic Landmark

SHM—State Historic Monument

SHS—State Historic Site

SHP—State Historical Park

SMem—State Memorial

SP—State Park

ALABAMA

1   **Arlington Home and Gardens,** 331 Cotton Ave., Birmingham 35211. The only surviving antebellum mansion in Birmingham, this Greek Revival plantation home was used in 1865 as a Union headquarters. Restored and furnished with 18th- and 19th-century antiques, the house stands amid six acres of landscaped gardens.

2   **First White House of the Confederacy,** 644 Washington St., Montgomery 36130. President Jefferson Davis and his family lived for a few months in this modest 1835 clapboard house while Montgomery—"Cradle of the Confederacy"—served as the Confederate capital. Period furnishings, family belongings, and war relics are displayed. The house was moved in 1920 to its present location opposite the State Capitol.

3   **Fort Morgan NHL,** Rte. 180, Gulf Shores 36542. Built in 1833, this star-shaped stronghold on the Gulf of Mexico is the nation's third largest fort. Seized by the Confederacy in 1861, it protected Mobile from the Union's blockading fleet until 1864, when the fort succumbed to Adm. David Farragut's all-out attack. Visitors tour the fort and a museum featuring weapons, maps, and uniforms.

4   **Horseshoe Bend NMP,** Rte. 1, Box 103, Daviston 36256. Twelve miles north of Dadeville, this 2,000-acre park, including a peninsula formed by a loop of the Tallapoosa River, preserves the site of Andrew Jackson's decisive victory over the Creek Indians in 1814. The battle brought Jackson national fame and opened the way for white settlement of southern Alabama and Georgia. Visitors study exhibits depicting phases of Indian culture, the Creek War, and pioneer life; follow a three-mile drive; and walk a three-mile nature-history trail.

5   **Tuskegee Institute NHS,** Tuskegee 36088. One of the first colleges for black Americans, Tuskegee was founded in 1881 by a former slaveholder and a former slave, and continues to educate students today. Booker T. Washington served as its first principal and president; his home is one of the original buildings still preserved. The Carver Museum, honoring Professor George Washington Carver, exhibits his experiments in crop diversification and agricultural science, as well as art displays and exhibits interpreting the history of the institute.

6   **U.S.S. *Alabama* Battleship Memorial,** Box 65, Mobile 36601. Now berthed in Mobile Bay, this ship earned nine battle stars in Pacific campaigns during World War II. Visitors tour decks, quarters, and wheelhouse, sit behind 40-mm anti-aircraft guns. Docked alongside, the submarine U.S.S. *Drum* also welcomes visitors aboard.

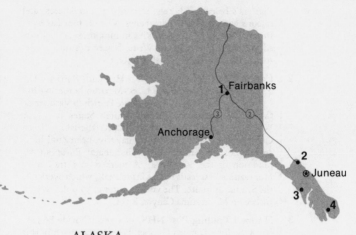

ALASKA

1 **Alaskaland-Pioneer Park,** Moore St. and Ave. of Flags, Fairbanks 99701. This state centennial park includes Gold Rush Town, a re-created, turn-of-the-century mining camp, and Mining Valley, where visitors see how miners panned for gold. A train takes visitors through the park to view a native village, moved from downtown Fairbanks when the city was built.

2 **Klondike Gold Rush NHP,** Skagway. Visitors relive the days of the last great gold rush at this 13,271-acre park. It includes historic buildings at Skagway, the Chilkoot and White Pass Trails, and an interpretive center in Seattle, Washington, where the S.S. *Portland* docked in July 1897 with two tons of Klondike gold, sparking a gold rush. Chilkoot Pass will be preserved for hikers who want to relive this arduous climb. Write: National Park Service, Pacific Northwest Regional Office, Fourth and Pike, Seattle, Washington 98101.

3 **Sitka NHP,** Box 738, Sitka 99835. Here the Tlingit Indians made their last stand against Russian fur traders and European domination in the 1804 Battle of Sitka. An outstanding collection of old totem poles line the trail between the visitor center and the Indians' fort site.

4 **Totem Bight SHS,** Totem Bight, Rte. 1, Box 719, Ketchikan 99901. More than a dozen fine totem poles depict legends of the Tlingit and Haida tribes. Visitors see a replica of a 19th-century community lodge, intricately carved and painted.

ARIZONA

1 **Bisbee.** Center of one of the richest copper-mining areas in America, Bisbee was a brawling mining camp in the 1880's. Steep Brewery Gulch and O.K. Street still boast that era's balconied hotels, miners' boardinghouses, and saloons with frosted windowpanes. Visitors tour Lavender Pit and Copper Queen mines. A mining museum is located in Copper Queen Plaza. Write: Bisbee Restoration Association, 37 Main St., Bisbee 85603.

2 **Coronado NMem,** Box 126, Hereford 85615. The 4,750-acre park lies on the U. S.-Mexican border within sight of the San Pedro Valley, where Francisco Vásquez de Coronado entered the present United States in 1540. While his expedition failed to discover the fabled Seven Golden Cities of Cíbola, which may have been Zuni Indian pueblos, it completed the first major European exploration of the Southwest. A marked foot trail from Montezuma Pass leads to Coronado Peak, which overlooks the Spaniards' route. The visitor center is 30 miles west of Bisbee on Montezuma Canyon Road.

3 **Hubbell Trading Post NHS,** Box 150, Ganado 86505. In 1878, John Lorenzo Hubbell became the owner of this post, the oldest still in operation on the Navajo Indian Reservation. The Hubbell home displays original furnishings, including Indian craft items and paintings. Hubbell encouraged Navajo handicrafts, particularly rugs and jewelry; they are still sold at the original sandstone trading post where Navajos and visitors shop for supplies. See book, page 327.

4 **Pioneer Arizona.** This 550-acre museum-village, 24 miles north of Phoenix, re-creates a late 19th-century settlement of the Southwest. Exhibits include houses, craft shops, a saloon, miners' camp, bank, schoolhouse, stagecoach stop, and an 1860 ranch with livestock. Write: Box 1677, Black Canyon Stage, Phoenix 85029.

5 **Pipe Spring NM,** Moccasin 86022. This 40-acre monument, 14 miles southwest of Fredonia on the Kaibab Indian Reservation, preserves an 1870's Mormon ranch house built like a fort. See book, page 258.

6 **San Xavier del Bac Mission NHL,** San Xavier Rd., Tucson 85706. Construction of this church, considered the most beautiful example of Spanish mission architecture in America, began in 1783. Today it is the center of a thriving parish on the San Xavier Papago Indian Reservation. See book, page 208.

7 **Tombstone NHL.** Tombstone sprang into existence when silver was discovered in the area, and it made its mark in the 1880's as a violent, lawless boomtown. Clustered in eight blocks around Allen St. are restored buildings of that era: the Bird Cage Theatre, a lusty frontier honky-tonk; the Crystal Palace Saloon; Tombstone Territorial Courthouse SHP; and the O.K. Corral stagecoach office and stables. Boothill Graveyard is on the northern edge of town. Write: Tombstone Information Center, Box 268, Tombstone 85638. See book, page 328.

8 **Tumacacori NM,** Box 67, Tumacacori 85640. The old frontier Mission of San José de Tumacacori lies 48 miles south of Tucson on I-19. The domed adobe church still stands, a stately baroque structure built around 1800 by Franciscans and Indian workmen. The unfinished bell tower is made of burned brick, and the interior shows the faded original colors applied by the Indians. Visitors tour the massive church, a walled cemetery with a round mortuary chapel, a modern museum housed in a mission-style building, and a patio garden.

9 **Yuma.** A key crossing point of the Colorado River from days of Spanish exploration, Yuma became a major transportation center and a lively boomtown during the gold rush. Emigrants passed by along the Gila River Trail. Fort Yuma, built for protection in 1850, lies on the California side of the river and is now tribal headquarters for the Quechan Indians. The 1876 Territorial Prison has been restored as a state historical park. Write: Chamber of Commerce, 377 Main St., Box 230, Yuma 85364.

ARKANSAS

1   **Arkansas Territorial Restoration,** Third and Scott Sts., Little Rock 72201. Thirteen buildings on their original sites within a half-block area re-create the Little Rock of the 1820's, when the frontier village became capital of Arkansas Territory. Among these homes, shops, and public buildings stands the oldest structure in the city—the Hinderliter Grog Shop, built in 1820 of hand-hewn oak logs and cypress siding. The Woodruff exhibit includes the home and printshop of the founder of the *Arkansas Gazette,* oldest continuously published newspaper west of the Mississippi.

2   **Fort Smith NHS,** Box 1406, Fort Smith 72902. Established as a military post in 1817 to keep the peace on the wild Louisiana Territory frontier, Fort Smith remained a center of law and order for 80 years. Foundations of the original wood fort can be seen, along with two buildings of the masonry fort that replaced it in 1838: the stone commissary, extensively restored; and the barracks, containing the restored courtroom where federal Judge Isaac Parker, the "hanging judge," presided from 1875 to 1896. Judge Parker appointed 200 deputy marshals; 65 were murdered. During his tenure Parker sentenced 181 men to the gallows, but only 79 were hanged. A replica of the gallows stands nearby.

3   **Old Washington Historic SP,** Box 98, Washington 71862. The tavern built here in 1824 at the junction of Fort Towson and the Southwest Trail was soon surrounded by a town, which served as Arkansas's capital during the Civil War. Notable visitors such as Davy Crockett and Sam Houston would feel at home in the reconstructed tavern. The 1841 courthouse and several homes have also been restored, along with the blacksmith shop where in 1831 James Black is supposed to have made the first Bowie knife, designed by Jim Bowie.

4   **Pea Ridge NMP,** U. S. 62, Pea Ridge 72751. The tardiness of their ammunition supply wagons helped defeat Confederate forces—including a thousand Cherokees—in a major battle here on March 7-8, 1862. With victory the Union gained undisputed control of Missouri. Exhibits describe the campaign. The park's 4,300 acres include a self-guiding auto tour and the restored Elkhorn Tavern, center of much of the fighting.

5   **Prairie Grove Battlefield SP,** Prairie Grove 72753. In December of 1862, Arkansas troops led by Gen. Thomas Hindman moved at a desperate pace across the mountains to cut off Union reinforcements. The two armies clashed at Prairie Grove on December 7. The arrival of more Union troops late in the day forced a Confederate retreat. Markers in this 130-acre park indicate battle lines; Hindman Hall Museum commemorates the battle. Nearby Vineyard Village re-creates an Ozark pioneer settlement of the early 1800's. Visitors tour a log home, farm buildings, school, and church.

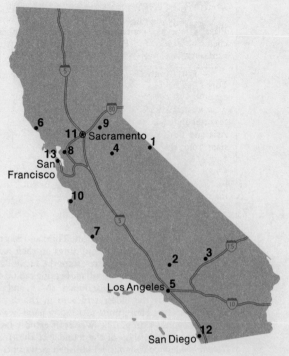

CALIFORNIA

1 | **Bodie SHP,** Box 515, Bridgeport 93517. After Waterman S. Body struck gold here in 1859, Bodie burgeoned into a tough mining camp notorious for saloons, street fights, robberies, and killings. In its heyday, Bodie attracted 10,000 residents and yielded 100 million dollars worth of gold. A ghost town, it today numbers 170 original buildings, preserved in a state of "arrested decay." The town's attractions include several old houses, a stamping mill, jail, schoolhouse, church, blacksmith shop, and museum. Bodie may be snowbound in winter; check road conditions before driving.

2 | **Burton's Tropico Gold Mine and Museum,** Mojave Tropico Rd., Rte 1, Box 101, Rosamond 93560. The Tropico Mine yielded millions of dollars worth of gold between 1894 and 1956. Visitors go on a guided tour underground and look down a 900-foot shaft to see how gold was mined. The museum and its annexes display relics of gold mining history and exhibits of the mine's "glory days."

3 | **Calico Ghost Town Regional Park,** Box 638, Yermo 92398. A silver boomtown between 1881 and 1897, Calico declined when the price of silver dropped. Now restored, the town features Maggie Mine, Lil's Saloon, miners' shacks, assay office, general store, firehouse, schoolhouse, cemetery, printshop, spice store, bottle shop, leather works, and museum.

4 | **Columbia SHP,** Box 151, Columbia 95310. One of the richest placer mining areas of the Mother Lode, Columbia boomed during the 1850-60 decade. Visitors today tour a gold mine, ride a stagecoach, see fire-fighting equipment, attend summer plays in the theater, and wander through reconstructed buildings scattered over a 12-block area. See book, page 333.

5 | **El Pueblo de Los Angeles SHP.** Much of Los Angeles' original Spanish settlement has been preserved or restored here. Attractions include the Franciscan Old Mission Church, oldest religious building in the city, erected in 1814 with the proceeds of California brandy sales; Olvera St., a typical Mexican village street with sidewalk shops and food stalls; Avila Adobe Museum, the oldest dwelling in Los Angeles, built about 1818, frequented by Kit Carson, and used as a government seat by Gen. John C. Frémont; the Old Spanish Plaza with its bronze statue of the city's founder, Governor Felipe de Neve; the 1884 Old Plaza Firehouse, containing its original pumper and chemical wagon; and Pico House, the city's first court-yarded three-story hotel. Write: Visitor Center, 622 N. Main St., Los Angeles 90012.

6   **Fort Ross SHP,** Rte. 1, Jenner 95450. Russian fur traders built a stockaded fort and trading post here in 1812 on what was then Spanish land. From this base they hunted sea otter and seal in coastal waters and shipped the pelts to Asia and Europe. After decimating the herds, the Russians sold the fort to Capt. John Sutter in 1841 for $30,000 in gold and produce. Restored within the 600-acre commemorative park are the redwood stockade, two blockhouses, a Russian Orthodox church, and the commandant's home—a Russian log house.

7   **Hearst San Simeon SHM.** Atop the 1,600-foot "Enchanted Hill" overlooking the Pacific Ocean stands the palatial estate of publisher William Randolph Hearst. The huge, Hispano-Moorish "castle," designed by architect Julia Morgan, and three guesthouses are filled with the Hearst family's magnificent art treasures and antiques, most of them baroque and medieval styles. Fountains and statues line the paths of a formal garden famous for its roses, exotic plants, and two grandiose pools: the marble Greco-Roman "Neptune Pool" and an indoor Roman bath with mosaic tiles that glitter with real gold. Write: San Simeon Region, Box 8, San Simeon 93452.

8   **John Muir NHS,** 4202 Alhambra Ave., Martinez 94553. Muir—the famed conservationist, naturalist, author, explorer, "father of the national parks," and a founder of the Sierra Club—lived in this late-Victorian mansion from 1890 until his death in 1914. Restored to its turn-of-the-century appearance, the house is filled with Muir memorabilia and period antiques, including his flat-topped desk. Also at the site stands an 1849 adobe ranch house with restored vineyards and orchards.

9   **Marshall Gold Discovery SHP,** Rte. 49, Coloma 95613. Visitors to the 280-acre commemorative park see a replica of the sawmill where James Marshall, partner of John Sutter, spotted the first flecks of California gold in 1848. Marshall's preserved wooden cabin and remains of other original town structures still stand. A museum houses gold rush relics and explains the metal's economic significance; a hilltop statue marks the grave of James Marshall. See book, page 319.

10   **Monterey Old Town SHP,** 210 Olivier St., Monterey 93940. The Vizcaíno-Serra Landing Site (commemorating the first explorer to land on the peninsula and the priest who built its original presidio and mission) and several restored buildings evoke Monterey's colorful heritage under Spanish, Mexican, and U. S. flags. The Old Custom House, the oldest government building west of the Rockies, is the site where Commodore Sloat raised the United States flag in 1846. Bales and boxes stand ready for inspection today as in the 1840's, with china, wines, cigars, tools, and furniture among the items on display. California's First Theater, converted from a lodging house in 1848, contains theatrical relics and presents old-time plays. Robert Louis Stevenson House, where the author wrote *Vendetta of the West,* contains diaries, manuscripts, first editions, personal effects, and family memorabilia. Larkin House and Casa Soberanes represent 19th-century "Monterey style" family residences, and the 1847 Pacific Building houses a museum of California history.

     The Royal Presidio Chapel, part of the Old Town NHL, is the only surviving example of 18th-century architecture in the city and the only remaining structure of the original Monterey Presidio.

11   **Sacramento.** Within the ten-block area of Old Sacramento NHL lies the original Sacramento, founded in 1849 by Sam Brannan and the son of Capt. John Sutter. It served as a commercial center during the California gold rush, became capital of the new state in 1854, then grew into a major transportation terminus for railroad, Pony Express, and riverboat traffic. Preserved in this waterfront district are many historic structures, including Pony Express buildings, a railroad depot, a theater, and shops.

At Sutter's Fort SHP, a reconstruction of the adobe fort built by Captain Sutter in 1839, visitors see prairie schooners, an ore wagon, and other pioneer and gold rush relics. See book, pages 319, 331.

Write: Sacramento Visitors Bureau, 1300 "I" St., Sacramento 95814.

12 **San Diego.** Old Town San Diego SHP preserves the Spanish colonial heritage of California's first permanent settlement. Several old houses and shops surrounding a plaza have been restored to their Mexican-period appearance. Among them: La Casa de Estudillo, an adobe dwelling built in 1827 by a well-to-do Spanish family; La Casa de Machado y Stewart, circa 1830, which includes a living history program of craft demonstrations; La Casa de Machado y Silvas, built about 1843; the 1865 Mason Street School, one of the oldest public schools in the country, now a museum; Seeley Stable, a reconstruction of an 1869 structure, now housing a collection of old vehicles and Western memorabilia; and the San Diego *Union* office, the small frame building where the first edition of the paper was published in 1868.

Mission San Diego de Alcalá, founded by Father Junípero Serra in 1769, was the first of nine established by the lame Franciscan priest along the Pacific Coast. Here California's first irrigation dams and ditches were built, its first olive and palm trees planted. Originally located in what is now Old Town, the mission was moved to its present location in 1774, rebuilt in 1780 after a devastating Indian attack, and fully restored in 1931. See book, page 230.

The bark *Star of India,* a 205-foot-long, iron-hulled square-rigger fitted with 19 sails, lies moored at the Embarcadero. Built in 1863, the oldest merchant ship afloat has been restored as a museum to depict the lives of seamen of more than a century ago.

Write: San Diego Convention and Visitors Bureau, Suite 824, Dept. 700, 1200 Third Ave., San Diego 92101.

13 **San Francisco.** Several historic buildings, relics, and sites reflect San Francisco's heritage from its Spanish founding through the notoriety of its gold rush days to its development into a thriving mercantile center. Mission Dolores, with its old cemetery, marks the site of the 1776 Franciscan mission from which the city grew. The 1886 Haas-Lilienthal House is filled with Victorian furnishings. Fort Point NHS, a restored Civil War fort, displays military artifacts from past wars. The Cable Car Barn, built about 1886, contains photographs of San Francisco and the city's first cable car, as well as gaslights, mounted car bells, wheel-winding cables, and other cable car workings. In Chinatown, the largest Chinese settlement outside Asia, attractions include the Kong Chow Temple, built in 1851; Old St. Mary's Church; and the Chinese Historical Society of America Museum, which documents the Chinese role in California's pioneer days.

San Francisco Maritime NP, a floating museum, recalls California's seafaring past. Restored vessels, moored to a pier near Fisherman's Wharf, represent types of ships developed for use on the West Coast: the double-end paddlewheel ferryboat *Eureka,* built in 1890, once the largest passenger ferry in the world; the *Alma,* an 1891 flatbottomed schooner for carrying hay and other bulky cargoes; the sleek, three-masted lumber schooner *C. A. Thayer,* designed in 1895; the steam-powered wooden schooner *Wapama,* built in 1915; and the *Hercules,* a turn-of-the-century steam tugboat, one of the last of her kind still afloat.

Write: San Francisco Convention and Visitors Bureau, Box 6977, San Francisco 94101.

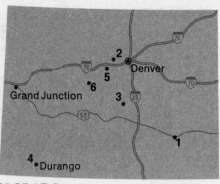

COLORADO

1   **Bent's Old Fort NHS,** 35110 Hwy. 194 East, La Junta 81050. Built by William Bent in 1833, this fortress made its impact on the history of the Southwest as a prosperous fur-trading post, rendezvous for trappers and Indians, way station on the Santa Fe Trail, and military base for the American conquest of New Mexico. Visitors tour the reconstructed fort and view craft demonstrations.

2   **Central City HD.** Colorado's first big gold strike was made here in 1859, and the town eventually became known as "the richest square mile on earth." Tourists explore old mines and visit the Teller House, an elegant frontier hostelry built at a cost of $107,000 in 1872. Write: Business Association, Box 456, Central City 80427. See book, page 340.

3   **Cripple Creek HD.** One of the richest gold camps of its day, Cripple Creek was famous for its saloons, dance halls, gambling and bawdy houses. Visitor sites include the old Midland Railroad Depot, now a museum; the former headquarters of the Western Federation of Mines; and the Imperial Hotel (1896), where an old-time melodrama is performed in the summer. Write: Chamber of Commerce, Box 307, Cripple Creek 80813. See book, page 331.

4   **Durango & Silverton Narrow-Gauge Railroad NHL.** Make reservations well in advance for this scenic trip between old mining towns in Victorian-era coaches pulled by steam locomotives. Write: Durango & Silverton Depot, 479 Main Ave., Durango 81301. See book page 342.

5   **Georgetown NHL.** After Colorado's first rich silver lode was discovered here, this community became the third largest city in the state. The only major camp not destroyed by fire, Georgetown retains about 200 original Victorian buildings. Hamill House (1867), built for a mining magnate, was the most luxurious home in Colorado. The Hotel de Paris (1875) was noted for its cuisine, ornate decor, and eccentric French owner. At nearby Georgetown Loop the tracks of the Colorado & Southern Railway switched back upon themselves up a steep gradient. A steam locomotive now carries passengers over a reconstructed section of the loop and the Devil's Gate Bridge. Write: The Georgetown Society, Inc., Box 667, Georgetown 80444.

6   **Leadville HD.** First a gold camp, Leadville became the silver-mining capital of Colorado in the 1870's. Restored buildings of that prosperous era include the Healy House, now a museum of fine Victorian furnishings, and millionaire James V. Dexter's log cabin, elaborately decorated inside. Tabor House was built by silver king H.A.W. Tabor, who also erected the popular Tabor Opera House. Here well-known performers of the day appeared, and Oscar Wilde once gave a lecture. The stage is still set for a performance. Tabor lost his fortune in the silver crash of 1893. Matchless Mine where he once made a million dollars a year and the cabin nearby where his widow, Baby Doe, died penniless may be visited. Write: Chamber of Commerce, Box 861, Leadville 80461.

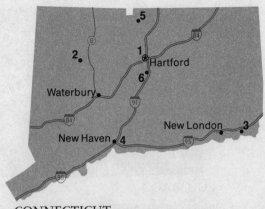

CONNECTICUT

1 **Hartford.** Connecticut's capital since 1662, Hartford preserves many historic buildings, including the State Capitol NHL and the Old State House NHL (1796), a Bulfinch masterpiece. The State Library displays the Colt Collection of Firearms. Homes of authors Harriet Beecher Stowe and Mark Twain are open at Nook Farm in the western part of Hartford. Write: Convention and Visitors Bureau, 1 Civic Center Plaza, Hartford 06103.

2 **Litchfield HD.** The historic district around the green and on North and South Sts. represents one of the finest examples of an original 18th-century New England town. Most houses are privately owned, but Tapping Reeve's 1773 home is open to the public. In a one-room building nearby he founded America's first law school in 1784. Graduates included two Vice Presidents and three Supreme Court justices. Litchfield also maintains a restored 1829 church and a museum on the green. Write: The Litchfield Division, Chamber of Commerce of Northwest Connecticut, Box 59, Torrington 06790.

3 **Mystic Seaport,** Mystic 06355. This popular maritime museum re-creates a typical 19th-century seafaring village with all the excitement—and fine craftsmanship—of the age of sail. See book, page 210.

4 **New Haven.** Yale University has been the city's cultural center since 1716. The Old Campus contains the university's oldest ivy-covered building, Connecticut Hall NHL, built in 1752. Memorial Quadrangle has Gothic-style buildings. Across College St. from Yale is the New Haven Green HD. Three churches are its only buildings, all built about 1815. Grove Street Cemetery holds the graves of Eli Whitney, Noah Webster, Roger Sherman, and other historic figures. Write: Chamber of Commerce, 195 Church St., New Haven 06506.

5 **Old New-Gate Prison,** Newgate Rd., East Granby 06026. Colonial America's first copper mine (1707) was turned into a prison for tories and others during the Revolutionary War. Some say that Benjamin Franklin's loyalist son William was imprisoned here. Old New-Gate served as Connecticut's state prison from the end of the war until 1827. Prisoners were chained in damp, unlighted rock caverns leading from the foot of the mine shaft. Visitors view the underground dungeons, the restored guardhouse, and ruins of prison buildings.

6 **Wethersfield.** Old Wethersfield HD, a picturesque New England village, contains the oldest restored house in town, the 1692 Buttolph-Williams House NHL. Other historic sites include the 18th-century Silas Deane House, the Isaac Stevens House, and the old meetinghouse. Washington and the Comte de Rochambeau planned the Yorktown campaign in the Joseph Webb House NHL (1752), an elegant colonial mansion. Write: Office of the Town Clerk, 505 Silas Deane Highway, Wethersfield 06109.

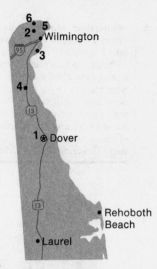

DELAWARE

1 **Dover.** Handsome homes and the Old State House grace Dover's green, laid out in 1717. The Hall of Records preserves historical documents. The Governor's Mansion, a brick house built about 1790, reportedly served as an Underground Railroad station. At the John Dickinson Plantation lived the "Penman of the Revolution," whose stirring tracts helped spur the patriot cause. Write: Division of Historical Affairs, Box 1401, Dover 19903.

2 **Hagley Museum,** Rte. 141, Wilmington 19807. Buses carry visitors around the 230-acre tract where Eleuthère Irénée du Pont founded his powder mills in 1802 near Wilmington. Dioramas and displays in an 1814 textile mill trace the evolution of American industry. Working models in the Millwright Shop illustrate the manufacture of gunpowder. About a mile away stands Eleutherian Mills, the first du Pont family residence, as well as a barn with antique vehicles and farm equipment, cooper shop, and the first office of the Du Pont Company.

3 **New Castle.** Narrow streets lined with brick homes enhance the charm of Delaware's colonial capital, founded by the Dutch in 1651. Amstel House, restored home of a Delaware governor, contains colonial furnishings. On the green, pegged out by Peter Stuyvesant in 1655, stands the Old Court House—colonial capitol, statehouse, then county seat; the Old Dutch House, probably the oldest brick dwelling in the state; the Arsenal, arms storehouse during the War of 1812 and the Mexican War; and Immanuel Church, Delaware's first Episcopal parish. Imported marble and finely carved woodwork embellish the George Read II House, a fine example of late-Georgian architecture. Write: New Castle Historical Society, New Castle 19720.

4 **Odessa HD.** Distinguished 18th- and 19th-century buildings reflect Odessa's years as a thriving grain-shipping center named after the Russian grain port. The Corbit-Sharp House, built in 1772 by a Quaker tanner, is noted for its spacious grounds, old kitchen, and regional Chippendale and Federal furnishings. A prosperous merchant added the main Georgian-style section of the Wilson-Warner House next door in 1769. The 1822 Brick Hotel Gallery, once a popular teamster stop, serves as an exhibition center. Write: Historic Houses of Odessa, Delaware, Box 507, Odessa 19730.

5 **Wilmington.** Fort Christina NHL commemorates the site of the first permanent European settlement in Delaware by Swedes in 1638. A typical log cabin (introduced to America by Swedish settlers) stands in the two-acre park. Holy Trinity Church, consecrated in 1699, is among the oldest Protestant churches still used for worship in North America. Write: Convention and Visitors Bureau, 1300 Market St., Wilmington 19801.

6 | Winterthur Museum, Rte. 52, Winterthur 19735. Henry Francis du Pont converted his family's homestead into a repository of American interior architecture, furnishings, and decorative accessories. Nearly 200 period settings and display areas record American domestic taste from 1640 to 1840. A parlor features furniture crafted by New York cabinetmaker Duncan Phyfe; pieces made by early Dutch settlers in the Hudson Valley furnish a bedroom. Other displays include Chinese porcelain and a hall of carved wooden statues. Du Pont landscaped Winterthur's flowering woods, parks, gardens, and a pine grove.

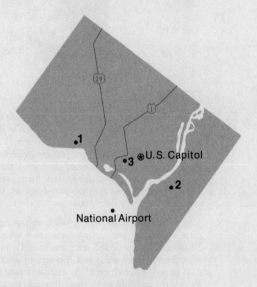

.1

.3 ⊕U.S. Capitol

.2

National Airport

DISTRICT OF COLUMBIA

1 | Chesapeake and Ohio Canal NHP. See Maryland.

2 | Frederick Douglass Home, 1411 W St., S.E., Washington, D. C. 20020. Born a slave in Maryland in 1818, Frederick Douglass became a prominent author, editor-publisher of an abolitionist newspaper, and crusader for human rights. While holding government posts, Douglass lived in this 21-room house, now filled with Victorian furnishings and personal mementos.

1 | Georgetown. Federal and Georgian town houses grace narrow, tree-lined streets in this fashionable residential area—once a colonial commercial center, today home of Georgetown University, oldest Catholic college in the nation. Old Stone House, refurbished with colonial furniture, sponsors craft demonstrations. The federal-style Dumbarton House features a typical garden of the 1800's. Formal gardens surround Dumbarton Oaks, scene of the 1944 meeting that led to formation of the United Nations. Write: Washington Tourist Information Center, 1400 Pennsylvania Ave., N.W., Washington, D. C. 20230.

National Capital Region. The National Park Service administers monuments, forts, houses, government buildings, and other historical properties in the District of Columbia, Virginia, and Maryland. Write: 1100 Ohio Dr., S.W., Washington, D. C. 20024. See book, page 379.

3 | Smithsonian Institution, Washington, D. C. 20560. Founded in 1846 with money willed by Englishman James Smithson, "the nation's attic" today encompasses art galleries, museums, and research facilities. The National Museum of American History celebrates American culture and inventive achievements, including Whitney's cotton gin and Franklin's printing press. The National Air and Space Museum displays famous "firsts" in aviation and space flight, ranging from the Wright *Flyer* and the *Spirit of St. Louis* to *Friendship* 7. See book, page 386.

FLORIDA

1 De Soto NMem, 75th St., N.W., Bradenton 33529. This 25-acre park on Tampa Bay near Bradenton commemorates the landing of Spanish explorer Hernando de Soto on May 30, 1539, with a party of 600 men and 220 horses. In search of rumored golden empires, de Soto's men trekked some 4,000 miles over a four-year period and discovered the Mississippi—the first major European exploration of the southeastern United States. De Soto died on the expedition. An audiovisual program outlines the explorer's remarkable accomplishments. Markers along a nature trail point out native plants and explain their use by Indians and European settlers.

2 John F. Kennedy Space Center, Merritt Island, near Titusville 32780. NASA administers the space center, the site of historic Apollo and Skylab launches and current space-shuttle activities. Neighboring Cape Canaveral Air Force Station, a development and test center, was the launch site for Mercury and Gemini manned space flights from 1961 to 1966. NASA offers daily bus tours of major facilities, leaving from the visitor center on Route 405, south of Titusville.

3 Key West. As the southernmost city of the continental United States, Key West has been an important military and naval base since the 1820's. Defended by Fort Zachary Taylor, Key West was the only Southern city controlled by the Union throughout the Civil War. Key West HD architecture combines Old World charm with Bahamian influence. The restored Audubon House, where naturalist John James Audubon worked in 1832, displays some of his original paintings. Ernest Hemingway's Spanish-colonial home preserves his memorabilia. Write: Chamber of Commerce, 402 Wall St., Key West 33040.

4 St. Augustine. Established in 1565, St. Augustine is the oldest continuously inhabited European settlement in the United States. The Old City retains much of its original Spanish flavor. San Agustín Antiguo HD comprises more than 50 restored or reconstructed buildings, including homes, craft shops, an inn, and a military hospital. The Cathedral of St. Augustine NHL overlooks the Plaza de la Constitución (1598), oldest public square in the country. Castillo de San Marcos NM, a massive fortress built between 1672 and 1695, broods over St. Augustine.

Fort Matanzas NM lies 14 miles south of the city, near the spot where Pedro Menéndez de Avilés slaughtered his French rivals in 1565. A ferry carries visitors to Rattlesnake Island to view the coquina limestone fort. Built by the Spanish in 1740-42, it guarded the southern approach to St. Augustine. Write: Visitor Information Center, 10 Castillo Dr., St. Augustine 32084. See book, page 23.

GEORGIA

1   **Andersonville NHS,** Andersonville 31711. Largest and most infamous of the Civil War prison camps, Andersonville—known officially as Camp Sumter—covered 27 acres. Though built to hold 10,000 prisoners, it was packed with as many as 32,000 at one time; more than 12,000 Union soldiers died here. Still visible within the stockade are holes dug by prisoners searching for fresh water or attempting to tunnel to freedom. The site commemorates the sacrifices of all American prisoners of war and includes the Andersonville National Cemetery.

2   **Chickamauga and Chattanooga NMP,** Fort Oglethorpe 30742. Four Civil War battlefields comprise this park in Georgia and Tennessee—Chickamauga, Lookout Mountain, Orchard Knob, and Missionary Ridge, scenes of struggles for control of the railroad center at Chattanooga. Point Park on Lookout Mountain's northern tip offers a sweeping view of the whole area. The Chickamauga visitor center houses a collection of American military arms, more than 350 weapons, and a display of Civil War light field artillery.

3   **Fort Frederica NM,** Rte. 9, Box 286-C, St. Simons Island 31522. James Oglethorpe established this fort in 1736 as a base for military operations against the Spanish in Florida. Abandoned after the conflict ended, the fort and its supporting town now lie in ruins. A film, exhibits, and dioramas based on archeological excavations help bring Frederica to life again. Nearby is the site of the 1742 Battle of Bloody Marsh, the turning point in the Anglo-Spanish struggle for control of the area.

4   **Fort Pulaski NM,** Box 98, Tybee Island 31328. Perched on Cockspur Island at the mouth of the Savannah River, Fort Pulaski, with moat and drawbridges, was the pride of military engineering until, in 1862, Union bombardment with newly developed rifled cannons proved that masonry forts had become obsolete. Exhibits recount the fort's history. Cannon projectiles are still embedded in its walls. The preserve also includes a monument to John Wesley, founder of Methodism, who landed here in 1736 after crossing the Atlantic Ocean on his mission to the American Indians.

5   **Kennesaw Mountain NBP,** Box 1167, Marietta 30061. Here on June 27, 1864, Confederate Gen. Joseph E. Johnston's 50,000 men dug in to stop Gen. William Sherman's 100,000 Union troops from reaching Atlanta. Through two weeks of skirmishes and two major battles, both sides suffered heavy losses. Sherman, unable to break the Confederate line, finally used a flanking movement to force his opponents to retreat. On July 2, Sherman's army continued its march to Atlanta. Drives and trails through the park's 2,880 acres pass gun emplacements, battle markers, and Confederate earthworks.

6 | **Little White House,** Warm Springs 31830. President Franklin D. Roosevelt built this unpretentious cottage in 1932 for his frequent visits to enjoy the nearby mineral springs, therapeutic for polio victims. The house is maintained as it was on the day Roosevelt died here in 1945, even to the unfinished portrait for which he was sitting. At the museum, displays and a film chronicle Roosevelt's life; personal papers and mementos are also exhibited.

7 | **New Echota Restoration,** Rte. 3, Calhoun 30701. In 1825 the Cherokee Nation, organized in a republican form of government, founded its short-lived capital four miles northeast of Calhoun. Thirteen years later the Cherokees were herded away to Oklahoma. One original building, a missionary's house, has been restored; others have been rebuilt. At the Print Shop, the first Indian newspaper, the *Cherokee Phoenix,* was printed both in English and in the Cherokee syllabary invented by Sequoyah. An old-time press and copies of the newspaper are displayed.

8 | **Savannah HD.** Founded in 1733, Savannah was Georgia's first town and first capital. Its 52 parks constitute a legacy from James Oglethorpe's original town plan. A wealth of historic buildings grace the city, including the 1815 Georgian-style Davenport House and the 1816 Owens-Thomas House, both furnished with period antiques. The Regency House, Juliette Gordon Low's birthplace in 1860, is maintained as a memorial to the founder of Girl Scouting in America. Factor's Walk follows the old waterfront, where cobblestone ramps were made with ballast from sailing ships. Fort Jackson, built in 1840, houses a museum of Georgia's maritime history. Write: Savannah Visitors Bureau, 301 West Broad St., Savannah 31499.

9 | **Stone Mountain Park,** Box 778, Stone Mountain 30086. Robert E. Lee, Jefferson Davis, and Stonewall Jackson dominate this 3,200-acre recreational-historical park from one of the world's largest carvings—the Confederate memorial on Stone Mountain's granite face. Park attractions include a restored antebellum plantation, demonstrations of early industries, a Civil War museum, steam railroad, and riverboat.

10 | **Westville Village,** Lumpkin 31815. Dozens of original buildings from various parts of Georgia were relocated to create this rural village of the 1850's. The culture and crafts of the period thrive at farmhouse and mansion, shops, church, general store. Blacksmiths, weavers, quilters, potters, and brickmakers are at work. Special events include the Fair of 1850 held each November.

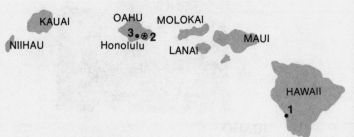

HAWAII

1 | **Pu'uhonua o Hōnaunau NHP,** Rte. 160, Honaunau, Kona 96726. This *puuhonua* (place of refuge) was established during the 15th century to give sanctuary to breakers of religious law, refugees in time of war, and defeated warriors seeking protection. War refugees remained until the conflict was over, taboo breakers until they had been purified by the priests who operated the refuge. Visitors today view a reconstructed temple-mausoleum and relics of the refuge's past on this six-acre lava shelf facing the Pacific. Guides in native costume demonstrate carving, weaving, and other crafts of early Hawaiians, and visitors can ride an outrigger canoe in a sparkling coral lagoon.

2 | Honolulu. Many of the historic treasures housed in the Bernice P. Bishop Museum were inherited by Princess Bernice Pauahi Bishop, the last direct descendant of Kamehameha the Great, the Hawaiian chief who unified the islands at the end of the 18th century. Visitors may see more than 10 million specimens of Pacific tropical flora, insects, and shells, as well as carved images of Hawaiian gods and detailed Hawaiian featherwork.

Iolani Palace, the only Royal palace in the United States, was occupied by Hawaii's last monarchs, King Kalakaua and his successor, Queen Liliuokalani, in the late 19th century. The throne room has been restored to its former grandeur, with replicas of the two original gilded thrones. The Iolani Barracks, a coral-block building that once housed the Royal guard, is also on the grounds. Queen Emma's Summer Palace, once a Royal mountain retreat, preserves relics of the Hawaiian monarchy. Furniture, clothing, and jewelry are exhibited with Hawaiian weapons, feather capes, and *leis*.

The Mission Houses and Kawaiahao Church commemorate the first Protestant missionary families who arrived from New England in 1820. In the church, Honolulu's oldest, King Kamehameha III supposedly uttered the words that became Hawaii's motto: "The life of the land is perpetuated in righteousness." Write: Chamber of Commerce, 735 Bishop St., Honolulu, Hawaii 96813.

3 | U.S.S. *Arizona* NMem, 1 Arizona Memorial Dr., Honolulu, Hawaii 96818. This battleship took a direct hit during the Japanese attack on Pearl Harbor in 1941; the bodies of most of the 1,177 crewmen are still entombed in the sunken hull. A memorial walkway spanning the vessel records names of the dead.

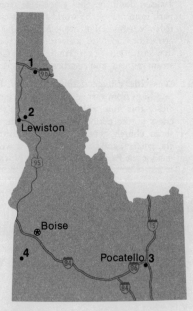

IDAHO

1 | Coeur d'Alene Mission of the Sacred Heart SHP, Box 135, Cataldo 83810. With simple tools and great perseverance, the Coeur d'Alene Indians in 1850 began to build this Greek Revival-style church under the supervision of Jesuit missionaries. From this outpost, the priests converted semi-nomadic Indian tribes of the region into Christian farmers. The mission, with its beautifully hand-carved altar, decorative ceiling panels, statues, and paintings, is preserved as Idaho's oldest building.

2 | Nez Perce NHP, Box 93 Spalding 83551. More than a score of historic and scenic sites in this 7,000-square-mile park 11 miles east of Lewiston commemorate the history and culture of the Nez Perce people and their country.

The park includes the site of the first mission among the Nez Perce and that of the first Indian agency, established in 1860; White Bird and Clearwater Battlefields, where Nez Perce warriors and U. S. Army troops fought during the Nez Perce War of 1877; Weippe Prairie NHL, where Lewis and Clark first encountered the Nez Perce; the town of Pierce, site of Idaho's 1860 gold strike; and Lolo Trail NHL and Pass over the Bitterroot Mountains, used by Lewis and Clark, and later by Nez Perce Indians and the U. S. Army during the Nez Perce War.

3   **Old Fort Hall Replica.** Several log dwellings, a blacksmith shop, and a museum, surrounded by a stout stockade, recall the role of Old Fort Hall in opening up the Pacific Northwest. Built in 1834 by adventurer Nathaniel Wyeth, the trading post grew into an important stopover for pioneers heading west on the Oregon Trail. Later it served as a trading post for miners rushing to goldfields in Idaho and Montana. Write: Dept. of Parks and Recreation, Box 4169, Pocatello 83205.

4   **Silver City.** Once queen of the nation's second largest silver-producing area, Silver City, with its permanent population of four, is now Idaho's largest and best-preserved old mining town. It includes some 70 early structures, among them the 1863 Idaho Hotel, furnished with period pieces, and the gingerbread-trimmed Stoddard House, built in the 1870's. Among the mines in the vicinity is the Ida Elmore. Its tunnels became the scene of underground warfare in 1868 when claim jumpers from the adjacent Golden Chariot Mine broke through into the Ida Elmore's workings. A gun battle outside the Idaho Hotel climaxed the "war." The town is situated high in the Owyhee Mountains; check road conditions before attempting any but mid-summer visits. Write: Box 75, Murphy 83650.

ILLINOIS

1 | **Bishop Hill HS,** U. S. 34, Bishop Hill 61419. This little-changed prairie utopia, founded by Swedish immigrants in 1846, preserves their original church, homes, and workshops. Internal wrangling and the murder of the founder ultimately doomed the colony. See book, page 228.

2 | **Chicago.** Fifteen years after the Great Fire of 1871 razed most of the city, architect Henry H. Richardson designed the 35-room Glessner House. Mansions of other millionaires also stand in the Prairie Avenue HD, being restored to its 19th-century appearance with gaslights and cobblestone streets. In 1889 pioneer social worker Jane Addams founded a settlement house for the poor—Hull House NHL. And during the 1880's George Pullman, the railroad sleeping car magnate, planned a model industrial community for his employees. The Florence Hotel, undergoing restoration, and more than 600 other buildings remain in the Pullman HD. Write: Convention and Tourism Bureau, McCormick Place, Chicago 60616.

3 | **Galena.** Riverboat traffic and nearby lead mines in the mid-1800's brought wealth to Galena, noted for its fine period architecture. The town gave the Union army nine Civil War generals, including Ulysses S. Grant, who clerked for his father in the J. R. Grant Leather Store. On his return from the war, the city presented the general with an Italianate brick dwelling—the Ulysses S. Grant Home SMem. Other attractions include a stockade used during the Black Hawk War; a 19th-century general store; John Dowling House, the city's oldest residence; and the Galena Historical Museum. Visitors also tour the nearby Vinegar Hill Lead Mine. Write: Chamber of Commerce, 101 Bouthillier St., Galena 61036.

4 | **Lincoln Heritage Trail Foundation,** Box 1809, Springfield 62705. A 2,200-mile marked highway links sites in three states associated with Abraham Lincoln's formative years. In Kentucky, where his parents married and he was born in 1809, Abe spent his earliest years. At age seven, he and his family moved to Indiana, where Abe attended school, borrowed books to read, and split rails. The Lincolns settled in Illinois in 1830. Here the young lawyer tried cases, married, debated Stephen A. Douglas, and entered the national political arena.

5 | **Lincoln's New Salem SHS,** Rte. 97, Petersburg 62675. Abraham Lincoln's hometown for six years has been restored as a frontier village with houses and shops. See book, page 310.

6 | **Nauvoo.** Restored buildings, including the homes of Joseph Smith and Brigham Young, recall the seven years when Nauvoo flourished as the principal settlement of the Mormons before their trek west in 1846. Write: Chamber of Commerce, Nauvoo 62354. See book, page 245.

7 | **Springfield.** In the heart of Lincoln country stands his home, law offices, tomb, and the Old State Capitol. Write: Convention and Visitors Bureau, 64 East Adams St., Springfield 62701. See book, page 314.

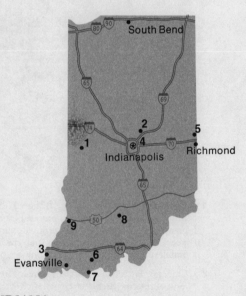

INDIANA

1 | **Billie Creek Village,** U. S. 36, Rockville 47872. Structures moved here from the local area capture the flavor of a prairie town: three covered bridges, schoolhouse, general store, pottery barn, and weaver's cottage. A farmstead includes animals and kitchen demonstrations.

2 | **Conner Prairie Pioneer Settlement,** Allisonville Rd., Noblesville 46060. Visitors learn about pioneer life of the 1830's at this 55-acre restoration. The village bustles with activity—a weaver dyes yarn, the smith hammers nails, the potter crafts a bowl, women quilt, weave baskets, cane chair seats, and gossip. Other interpreters and craftsmen work the fields and practice such forgotten arts as log-facing, processing flax, candle dipping, and soapmaking. William Conner's brick home (1823) illustrates the gracious life of a successful farmer-merchant. Daily activities revolve around the loom house, barn, brick kiln, stillhouse, and springhouse.

3 | **Historic New Harmony,** North at Arthur St., New Harmony 47631. Two distinct 19th-century experiments in communal living blend in a restoration that spans 200 years of Indiana history. See book, page 224.

4 | **Indianapolis.** The Benjamin Harrison Memorial Home, Italianate residence of the 23rd President (1889-93) until his death in 1901, contains his White House desk, personal mementos, and Mrs. Harrison's gowns. The James Whitcomb Riley Home has been preserved as it was when the popular Hoosier poet lived here and wrote many of his humorous and sentimental poems. Handcarved woodwork and marble fireplaces adorn the brick house. Write: Convention and Visitors Association, 200 South Capitol St., Indianapolis 46225.

5 | **Levi Coffin House NHL,** U. S. Box 77, Fountain City 47341. Between 1826 and 1846 Quaker abolitionist Levi Coffin and his wife Catharine helped some 2,000 runaway slaves escape to freedom in Canada. Tradition says that the Coffins sheltered Eliza Harris, whose real-life escape across the ice-clogged Ohio River inspired *Uncle Tom's Cabin.* Seventeen fugitives could hide at one time in the eight-room brick house, dubbed the Grand Central Station of the Underground Railroad.

6 | **Lincoln Boyhood NMem,** Rte. 162, near Gentryville. A living historical farm portrays pioneer life as Abraham Lincoln knew it here from 1816 to 1830. Write: Superintendent, Lincoln City 47552. See book, page 308.

7 | **Lincoln Pioneer Village,** City Park, Rockport 47635. This reconstructed village is dedicated to Abraham Lincoln and the 14 years he lived in Indiana. Buildings include replicas of the Lincoln Homestead and Old Pigeon Baptist Church, which Abe helped build. Lincoln earned 25 cents a day working for James Gentry, whose mansion is furnished with period pieces. Visitors also examine the home of Azel Dorsey, one of Lincoln's teachers, and John Pitcher's law office, to which Abe walked 17 miles to borrow law books. Museums house exhibits of pioneer items and early transportation.

8 | **Spring Mill Village,** Spring Mill SP, Rte. 60, Mitchell 47446. A restored frontier village mirrors pioneer life in the early and mid-1800's. A 24-foot waterwheel furnishes power for the sawmill and three-story gristmill, which grinds corn into meal. Visitors also see a hat factory, distillery, tavern, apothecary, chapel, general store, pioneer homes, and a pioneer garden.

9 | **Vincennes.** Indiana's oldest city, Vincennes was founded by the French as a trading post in 1683, renamed Fort Sackville by the British in 1763. Its capture by George Rogers Clark in 1779 during the Revolutionary War opened the Northwest Territory to American settlement. From 1800 to 1813 the Indian Territory was governed from a two-story frame house, the Indiana Territorial Capitol. Next to the capitol stands a reconstruction of the newspaper and printing office that housed the territory's first press. While territorial governor, William Henry Harrison built Grouseland, a Georgian-style house that now displays family portraits and furnishings of the 9th President (1841). Write: Chamber of Commerce, 417 Busseron St., Vincennes 47591.

IOWA

1 **Amana Colonies,** Amana 52203. These seven villages, all but one settled in 1855 by German Inspirationists, were among the most successful of the utopian communities attempted in the mid-19th century. Located within a 20-mile area, the villages retain much of their Old World character. See book, page 227.

2 **Bentonsport HD.** Mid-19th-century homes, stores, and buildings preserve the flavor of steamboat days on the Des Moines River. Historic sites include the English Renaissance-style post office built in 1852; the largest country store in Iowa, laden with old merchandise and fixtures; and the only steamboat hotel on the Des Moines River, the luxurious 1846 Mason House, with original furnishings that include the maple-and-walnut bar at which river captains hoisted glasses while swapping tales. Write: Bentonsport Improvement Assn., Keosauqua 52565.

3 **Fort Atkinson SMem,** Fort Atkinson 52144. Iowa's only surviving pioneer fort was built in 1840 to protect Winnebago Indians from nearby tribes. Portions of the barracks, two blockhouses, and a powder magazine still stand. The cannon house, stockade, officers' quarters, and parade grounds have been reconstructed.

4 **Fort Dodge Historical Museum and Fort,** Fort Dodge 50501. This site includes a replica of the fort built to protect settlers from hostile Sioux Indians during the 1862 uprising, a one-room schoolhouse, general store, log church, jail, blacksmith shop, and a museum displaying the area's historical artifacts.

5 **Herbert Hoover NHS,** Box 607, West Branch 52358. Within the 187-acre park stands the restored and refurnished birthplace cottage of Herbert Clark Hoover, a mining engineer who became the 31st President of the United States (1929-33); a replica of his father's blacksmith shop with antique tools; the restored Quaker meetinghouse that the Hoover family attended; the graves of President and Mrs. Hoover; and the Herbert Hoover Presidential Library and Museum, with documents and memorabilia representing his 50 years of public service as an administrator.

6 **Living History Farms,** 2600 N.W. 111th St., Des Moines 50322. The 500-acre site includes a working 1840 pioneer farm with log cabin and outbuildings; the Flynn Mansion, representative of the 1870's; a horse farm of 1900 vintage; and a museum containing agricultural implements and displays of farming methods. Demonstrations include blacksmithing, quilting, spinning, and weaving, as well as pioneer farming techniques.

7 **Pella Historical Restoration Site,** 507 Franklin St., Pella 50219. Twenty restored buildings filled with antiques commemorate the Dutch who settled here in 1847. As a child, Western lawman Wyatt Earp lived in the brick Van Spancheren House, built in 1849. Visitors see Dutch costumes, a collection of Delftware, a country store with historical artifacts, farmhouse, church, pottery and blacksmith shops, a log cabin, operating gristmill, and a craft shop where wooden shoes are still made. A tulip festival is held the second week of each May.

8 **Vesterheim,** 502 W. Water St., Decorah 52101. Nine historic buildings trace the history of Norwegian immigrants in the Midwest and display samples of their arts, handicrafts, household furnishings, and culture. Exhibits include a three-room Norwegian house, a one-room Iowan pioneer cabin, an operating blacksmith shop, and a stone mill. Much of the handmade furniture is decorated with rosemaling, the colorful Norwegian folk technique of painting on wood.

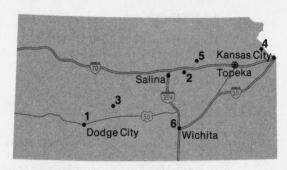

KANSAS

1 **Dodge City,** Dodge City 67801. Wild West make-believe recalls the heritage of a town that reigned as the world's largest cattle market in the 1800's. See book, page 345.

2 **Dwight D. Eisenhower Center,** S.E. Fourth and Buckeye Sts., Abilene 67410. The 20-acre complex commemorates the World War II commander of Allied forces in Europe and the nation's 34th President (1953-61). The Eisenhower Home, where "Ike" spent his boyhood, is kept as it was in 1946; the adjacent museum houses objects related to his life. The Presidential library contains papers, films, tapes, and photographs from his years as a soldier and President. A small chapel called the Place of Meditation holds the graves of Eisenhower, his wife, Mamie, and their son, Doud, who died at the age of three.

3 **Fort Larned NHS,** Rte. 3, Larned 67550. In the 1860's and early 1870's, Fort Larned served as an important military post on the Santa Fe Trail, and as a key fort during the Plains Indians campaigns. Before it was abandoned in 1878, the fort hosted Generals Hancock, Sherman, and Sheridan, as well as George Armstrong Custer, "Buffalo Bill" Cody, "Wild Bill" Hickok, and Kit Carson. Nine of the fort's original sandstone buildings, including the officers' quarters, two enlisted men's barracks, a quartermaster warehouse, two storehouses, and workshops, have been restored to their 19th-century condition.

4 **Fort Leavenworth,** Fort Leavenworth 66027. Established in 1827 to protect wagon trains on the Oregon and Santa Fe Trails, the post served for 30 years as a major base of operations on the Indian frontier. Visitors see a national cemetery and a museum displaying horse-drawn vehicles, including a 1790 Conestoga wagon and a sleigh that belonged to George Armstrong Custer. The fort also contains the state's oldest house, The Rookery, built in 1832.

5 **Fort Riley,** Fort Riley 66442. Headquarters of the 7th Cavalry and Lt. Col. George Armstrong Custer, the fort dates from 1853. Original buildings include officers' quarters; the first State Capitol, where the Kansas territorial legislature met in 1855; and the U. S. Cavalry Museum, first used as a post hospital and later as post headquarters.

6 **Historic Wichita Cowtown,** Wichita 67203. This 17-acre restoration site includes the city's first permanent house and church, Wyatt Earp's jail, period antiques, and a museum.

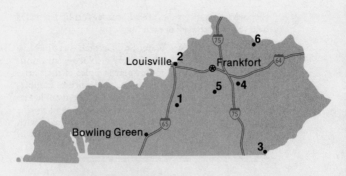

KENTUCKY

1 | **Abraham Lincoln Birthplace NHS,** Rte. 1, Hodgenville 42748. A colonnaded granite-and-marble memorial encloses the humble one-room log cabin that symbolizes Lincoln's birthplace at Sinking Spring farm. The limestone spring still flows; nearby stands the remains of the white oak tree that served as a boundary marker in Lincoln's day. The visitor center offers a film program and exhibits including a Bible that belonged to Lincoln's father.

2 | *The Belle of Louisville,* Louisville 40202. Whistle blowing, calliope on full, this triple-decker stern-wheeler cruises the Ohio River as proudly as she did on her maiden voyage in 1914. Steamboats have plied these waters since 1811. *The Belle,* one of the last of her kind, continues the tradition each summer with day-long excursions.

3 | **Cumberland Gap NHP,** Box 1848, Middlesboro 40965. The rugged Allegheny Mountains blocked the westward spread of colonists until 1750, when Dr. Thomas Walker, surveying a land grant, discovered the Indian Warriors' Path through Cumberland Gap. In 1775 Daniel Boone led a company of 30 men in blazing the Wilderness Road, opening Kentucky to settlement. U. S. 25E now cuts through the Gap. The 20,000-acre park, extending into Virginia and Tennessee, offers a visitor center-museum and roads to overlooks and historic sites, including Civil War fortifications. Fifty miles of trails trace steep ridges and dark wooded hollows. See book, page 192.

4 | **Fort Boonesborough SP,** Richmond 40475. The first frontier outpost on this site near the Kentucky River was built in 1775 by Daniel Boone and his pioneers after their arduous trek through Cumberland Gap. The reconstruction includes three furnished cabins, a trading post, and demonstrations of 18th-century crafts such as cabinetmaking, weaving, basketmaking, and blacksmithing.

5 | **Harrodsburg HD.** The oldest permanent English settlement west of the Alleghenies, Harrodsburg was founded in 1774 by 30 pioneers led by Capt. James Harrod. Buildings of widely varied architectural styles are preserved, including stone houses built in 1790. Old Fort Harrod SP features a museum of Kentucky history, a pioneer cemetery, and a reconstruction of the stockade, with blockhouse, cabins, and school. Write: Chamber of Commerce, Harrodsburg 40330.

5 | **Shakertown at Pleasant Hill NHL,** 3500 Lexington Rd., Harrodsburg 40330. This restored 19th-century Shaker village features dwellings and craft displays. See book, page 220.

6 | **Washington HD.** Founded in 1785 along the Indian trail into frontier Kentucky, the town of Washington grew to become, by 1797, a thriving commercial center. Fires and cholera reversed the town's fortunes. Main Street remains little changed. Among the restored buildings are an original log cabin; the 1789 Broderick's Tavern, still offering hospitality; and Mefford's Station, a house built from the planks of the flatboat that brought Mefford's family here on the Ohio River from Pittsburgh. Write: Old Washington, Inc., Rte. 2, Maysville 41056.

LOUISIANA

1 | **Chalmette NHP**, St. Bernard Hwy., Chalmette 70043. Gen. Andrew Jackson led his troops to victory over British forces here on January 8, 1815, at the Battle of New Orleans, two weeks after the War of 1812 had ended. Markers and cannons indicate the line of fire where Kentucky rifles shattered Gen. Edward Pakenham's army. A visitor center is located on the site. See book, page 198.

2 | **Fort Jackson**, Rte. 23, Buras 70041. After a nine-day siege in 1862, this star-shaped fort fell to Union naval forces under Admiral Farragut, leading to the capture of New Orleans. A museum within the restored fort contains relics; field markers retell the fort's history.

3 | **Plantation Homes** along the Mississippi River and its bayous from New Orleans to St. Francisville recall the days when cotton and cane sugar reigned. Write: Louisiana Office of Tourism, Box 94291, Baton Rouge 70804. See book, page 278.

1 | **Vieux Carré HD.** This oldest section of New Orleans glories in narrow streets, flower-filled courtyards, and Creole homes with wrought-iron balconies. Most of the structures, fusions of Greek Revival, French, and Spanish styles, were built between 1794 and 1850. Several buildings can be visited, including the Ursuline Convent. Write: Greater New Orleans Tourist and Convention Commission, 1520 Sugar Bowl Dr., New Orleans 70112.

MAINE

1 | **Maine Maritime Museum**, 963 Washington St., Bath 04530. The maritime history of Maine since 1607, emphasizing the 19th-century sailing ship era, is traced here, at the Winter Street Center, and at Sewall House. The museum also runs a traditional boatbuilding apprentice shop. The Percy & Small Shipyard NHS has been restored to its turn-of-the-20th-century condition with five original buildings. Once a producer of six-masted schooners, the yard is now the scene of shipbuilding and restoration.

2   **Portland.** The architecture of Portland's Spring Street HD reflects the wealth of a shipping center that has survived since colonial days. Houses include the federal-style McLellan-Sweat Mansion, built in 1800, and the Victorian Morse-Libby House, which features a mahogany flying staircase with more than 300 handcarved balusters. The Tate House, built in 1775, is the restored residence of George Tate, mast agent for Britain's Royal Navy. The Wadsworth-Longfellow House, childhood home of poet Henry Wadsworth Longfellow, was built by his grandfather in 1785. Write: Chamber of Commerce, 142 Free St., Portland 04101.

3   **Roosevelt Campobello International Park,** Campobello Island, near Lubec 04652. Franklin D. Roosevelt summered here from his earliest years until he was stricken with polio in 1921. The 34-room Dutch colonial "cottage" is furnished almost as it was when his family occupied it after 1910. A few mementos of his White House years have been added. Trails, picnic spots, and scenic lookout points lace the 3,000-acre park.

4   **York.** York Village provides a peaceful, informal setting for its mellow colonial houses, church, and cemetery. Homes on display include the Elizabeth Perkins House and the Emerson-Wilcox House (1740). The Old York Gaol is one of the oldest public buildings in English-settled America. Begun about 1719, it served as a prison until 1860. Visitors tour its gloomy dungeon and view the gaoler's living quarters, restored to their 1790 appearance. Nearby stands the John Hancock Warehouse, once owned by that signer of the Declaration of Independence. The Jefferds Tavern has been reconstructed and restored. Write: The Old York Historical Society, York 03909.

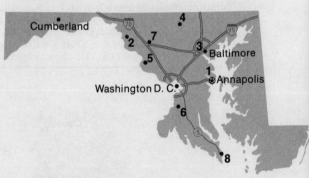

MARYLAND

1   **Annapolis HD.** One of the nation's earliest planned cities, Annapolis has been Maryland's capital since 1694 and briefly served as the nation's capital after the Revolution. In 1784 the Continental Congress met in the lofty State House, the nation's oldest in continuous use, to ratify the treaty of peace with Great Britain. Many restored Georgian homes and buildings are open to visitors, including the 1774 Hammond-Harwood House, considered a masterpiece of this style. Much of the 18th-century waterfront is preserved. A visit to the U. S. Naval Academy, established here in 1845, includes a tour of a museum of naval history. Write: Chamber of Commerce, 652 Main St., Annapolis 21401. See book, page 81.

2   **Antietam NB,** Box 158, Sharpsburg 21782. These gently rolling fields were strewn with dead and wounded soldiers on September 17, 1862, when the day-long Civil War Battle of Antietam brought staggering losses to both

Union and Confederate armies. Neither side won, but Gen. Robert E. Lee was stopped in his first attempt to enter the North. Exhibits and audio-visual programs describe the campaign; visitors follow the battle along eight miles of tour road. See book, page 273.

3 | **Baltimore.** An important seaport and industrial city since 1729, Baltimore preserves many historic neighborhoods and buildings, including the nation's oldest Catholic cathedral and third oldest synagogue. Restored Carroll Mansion was the home of Charles Carroll, signer of the Declaration of Independence. At the Mother Seton House, America's first native-born canonized saint founded the American Sisters of Charity in 1809. At Flag House, Mary Pickersgill made the flag that flew over Fort McHenry. The B & O Railroad Museum features replica and original locomotives, such as the *Tom Thumb*. The frigate *Constellation,* one of the nation's oldest warships, built in Baltimore in 1797, is now a floating maritime museum at the downtown waterfront. Write: Greater Baltimore Committee, 2 Hopkins Plaza, Baltimore 21201.

4 | **Carroll County Farm Museum,** Westminster 21157. A small farm typical of 1850 has been restored on this 140-acre tract, with furnished farmhouse and a barn and outbuildings containing early tools and implements. Blacksmithing, spinning, weaving, and other home crafts are demonstrated in special programs.

5 | **Chesapeake and Ohio Canal NHP.** Begun in 1828, this canal parallels the Potomac River and until 1924 transported goods between Cumberland, Maryland, and Washington, D. C., a distance of 184 miles. Hikers and bikers along the towpath pass locks, lockhouses, and aqueducts. Leisurely excursions by mule-drawn barge are offered in summer at the Washington end. Visitor centers are located at Great Falls Tavern, Hancock, and Cumberland. Write: Box 4, Sharpsburg 21782.

3 | **Fort McHenry NM and Historic Shrine,** Baltimore 21230. In 1776 patriots hastily erected a fort on strategic Whetstone Point to protect Baltimore from British ships. In the 1790's a permanent star-shaped stronghold was built on the site and served as an active military post for 100 years. During the War of 1812, Fort McHenry withstood bombardment for 25 hours before the British gave up and withdrew their forces. The American victory inspired Francis Scott Key to write "The Star-Spangled Banner," adopted as our national anthem in 1931. Visitors tour the fort's bastions, barracks, and batteries.

6 | **Fort Washington Park,** Indian Head Highway, Ft. Washington, 20021. The first fort at this site across the Potomac from Mount Vernon was built in 1809 to defend the new nation's Capital. Destroyed during the War of 1812, the fort was replaced in 1824 with the present masonry fortress. Daily tours of the fort are offered, with military demonstrations Sundays.

7 | **Frederick.** Founded in 1745, Frederick is now, as it was then, the seat of a largely agricultural county. From Frederick in 1765 came the first rebellion against the Stamp Act. A hundred years later, Frederick paid $200,000 to Confederate Gen. Jubal Early to ransom the town from burning. Historic buildings include the home and glove shop of Barbara Fritchie, legendary heroine of the Civil War; the home of Roger Brooke Taney, the Supreme Court Justice who handed down the Dred Scott decision; and Rose Hill Manor, home of Maryland's first elected governor, Thomas Johnson. His grave, along with those of Francis Scott Key and Barbara Fritchie, may be seen at Mount Olivet Cemetery. Write: Visitor Information Center, 19 East Church St., Frederick 21701.

8 | **St. Mary's City.** Replica statehouse and numerous exhibits, including a full-rigged ship, attract visitors to the state's first settlement and its capital until 1694. Write: Box 39, St. Mary's City 20686. See book, page 19.

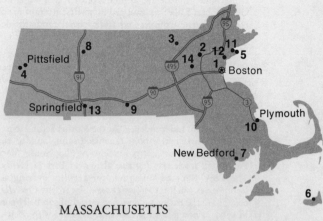

MASSACHUSETTS

1   **Adams NHS,** 135 Adams St., Quincy 02169. Built in 1731, the "Old House" was home to four generations of the Adams family from 1788 to 1927. John Adams retired here after his Presidency (1797-1801), and his son, John Quincy Adams, 6th President (1825-29), used it as a summer home. Grandson, diplomat Charles Francis Adams, and great-grandsons, historians Henry and Brooks Adams, also lived in the house, which preserves family furnishings. The stone library next door, built in 1870 by Charles Francis Adams, contains the books that belonged to President John Quincy Adams.

1   **Boston.** The Freedom Trail, a marked walking tour through downtown Boston, leads visitors to major Revolutionary War sites. In addition to more famous landmarks, the trail passes the Old Granary Burial Ground, where tombs of prominent patriots and other citizens may be seen, and King's Chapel, the first Anglican church in New England. See book, page 143.

Boston NHP combines six significant Revolutionary War sites—some of them on the Freedom Trail—with the Charlestown Navy Yard. The U.S.S. *Constitution,* famous for victories over French privateers, Barbary pirates, and British warships, lies berthed at the navy yard. Paul Revere fashioned the copper bolts and fittings for *"Old Ironsides."* See book, page 207.

Other Boston sites include the Common and adjacent Beacon Hill, the elegant "Brahmin" residential area, famed for its federal-style architecture. Boston's talented architect, Charles Bulfinch, designed several houses here, notably three for Harrison Gray Otis from 1795 to 1808. The first, at 141 Cambridge St., is open to the public. Write: Convention and Visitors Bureau, Box 490, Prudential Plaza, Boston 02199.

1   **Cambridge.** World-famous universities—Harvard, Radcliffe, and the Massachusetts Institute of Technology—enliven this old town. Harvard, founded in 1636, is the oldest university in the United States, and its historic "Yard" displays architecture ranging from colonial to contemporary. The oldest building, Massachusetts Hall NHL, was erected in 1720. Daniel Chester French's idealized statue of John Harvard stands outside University Hall NHL (1813-15), designed by Charles Bulfinch.

Cambridge is rich in Revolutionary War history. Christ Church NHL, built in 1761, quartered colonial soldiers; its organ pipes were melted down for bullets. A bronze tablet marks the spot on Cambridge Common where Washington is said to have taken command of the Continental army on July 3, 1775. His headquarters during the siege of Boston later became Henry Wadsworth Longfellow's home from 1837 to 1882. The poet wrote his most famous works in this three-story mansion, now preserved as the Longfellow NHS. Write: City Hall, 795 Massachusetts Ave., Cambridge 02139.

2   **Concord.** The 750-acre Minute Man NHP, stretching along the redcoats' route between Lexington and Concord, commemorates the beginning of the Revolutionary War. Costumed citizens each year observe the anniversary of the April 19, 1775, battle with British soldiers at Old North Bridge. See book, page 151.

Concord's literary landmarks include Ralph Waldo Emerson's white brick house, built in 1820; Nathaniel Hawthorne's Old Manse; and Orchard House, where Louisa May Alcott began writing *Little Women*. Walden Pond is preserved in a 150-acre state reservation, but Henry David Thoreau's cabin is gone. All these writers lie buried in Sleepy Hollow Cemetery. Write: Chamber of Commerce, ½ Main St., Concord 01742.

3 **Fruitlands Museums SHL**, Prospect Hill, Harvard 01451. This 18th-century farmhouse, home of Bronson Alcott's transcendentalist community, is one of a complex of four museum buildings. Another, a Shaker house built in the 1790's at the former Harvard Shaker Village, features their handicrafts. See book, page 228.

4 **Hancock Shaker Village NHL**, Box 898, Pittsfield 01201. Founded in 1790, the village remained active until 1960. Buildings, tools, and furniture show the simplicity and elegance of design for which the Shakers were famous. The 1826 round stone barn was constructed with three working levels to save labor.

1 **John Fitzgerald Kennedy NHS**, 83 Beals St., Brookline 02146. The 35th President (1961-63) was born in this suburban Boston home on May 29, 1917, and lived here until the age of three. His mother, Mrs. Rose Kennedy, supervised the restoration of the house to its 1917 appearance. Many of her belongings are preserved here, and a recording relates her personal memories.

2 **Lexington.** On April 19, 1775, the first Revolutionary War skirmish pitted some 70 Lexington militiamen against 700 Concord-bound redcoats on Lexington green. Each April sees a costumed re-enactment of the confrontation, and the visitors' center displays a diorama of the event. Write: Lexington Visitors Center, 1875 Massachusetts Ave., Lexington 02173. (See Concord entry for Minute Man NHP.) See book, page 148.

5 **Marblehead.** Settled in the 1620's as a fishing community, Marblehead strongly supported the Revolution. The 18th-century residential area boasts many houses associated with that war. Visitors stroll the narrow streets of history and legend, and admire the popular "Spirit of '76" painting by A. M. Willard in Abbot Hall. Legend holds that a corner of the Lafayette House was cut away to allow Lafayette's carriage to pass by during a visit in 1824. Two beautifully restored 18th-century dwellings are on view: the Jeremiah Lee Mansion and "King" Hooper Mansion. Pre-Revolutionary sites include a fort, a circular powder house, an old burial ground, and one of the oldest Episcopal churches in New England, St. Michael's, which dates from 1714. Write: Chamber of Commerce, 62 Pleasant St., Marblehead 01945. See book, page 212.

6 **Nantucket HD.** World's leading whaling port until the 1820's, Nantucket preserves many houses built before 1850. These range from the island's oldest, the Jethro Coffin House (1686), through a typical house of 1800, to the Hadwen House-Satler Memorial, a Greek Revival-style mansion of the 1840's. A whaling museum contains outstanding exhibits of the town's seafaring days. Visitors also tour an old "gaol," a mill, the Quaker meetinghouse, and the home of Maria Mitchell, the nation's first woman astronomer. Write: Nantucket Public Relations Committee, 25 Federal St., Nantucket 02554. See book, page 216.

7 **New Bedford District NHL.** Historic buildings have been restored in the town's waterfront area, heart of the country's whaling industry from the 1820's to the Civil War. Leading examples include the Seamen's Bethel (1832), the whaleman's chapel Herman Melville attended and immortalized in *Moby Dick;* the 1787 Mariner's Home, once a boardinghouse for sailors and still a seamen's shelter; the Old Bank (1831); and the U. S. Customhouse (circa 1835). The Whaling Museum boasts a superb collection of whaling relics, including a half-scale model of the whaler *Lagoda* which visitors can board. Write: Old Dartmouth Historical Society, Whaling Museum, 18 Johnny Cake Hill, New Bedford 02740. See book, page 216.

8 **Old Deerfield Village NHL.** A frontier town settled by the English in 1669, Deerfield suffered two violent attacks by French and Indians, but recovered to become a prosperous farming and cattle-raising community before the Revolution. Historic houses lining the mile-long main street date from colonial times to the early 19th century. Among them are homes with Early American antiques, a silversmith's workshop and silver collection, two taverns, and Frary House, where Benedict Arnold is said to have stopped on his way to attack Fort Ticonderoga. The Textile Museum, a Victorian barn, contains a remarkable display of costumes, needlework, and textiles from the 17th to 19th centuries. Write: Historic Deerfield, Inc., Box 321, Deerfield 01342. See book, page 71.

9 **Old Sturbridge Village,** Sturbridge 01566. More than 40 New England buildings have been moved here to re-create a farming community of the early 1800's. Homes and a general store border the village common, which is dominated by a white-steepled meetinghouse. Men and women in period dress demonstrate barrel making and other early 19th-century crafts and skills. The village includes a working farm.

10 **Plymouth.** Site of the first Pilgrim settlement in the New World, Plymouth boasts the *Mayflower II* and Plymouth Rock, as well as early dwellings and Pilgrim Hall museum. Plimoth Plantation nearby re-creates the settlement as it may have looked in 1627. Write: Chamber of Commerce, 85 Samoset St., Plymouth 02360. See book, page 48.

11 **Salem.** First town in the Massachusetts Bay Colony, Salem became famous for witchcraft trials and worldwide maritime trade. Buildings associated with both eras still stand. Write: Chamber of Commerce, 32 Derby Sq., Salem 01970. See book, pages 61, 216.

12 **Saugus Iron Works NHS,** 244 Central St., Saugus 01906. America's first successful ironworks has been rebuilt in its original setting on the banks of the Saugus River. See book, page 65.

13 **Springfield.** Springfield Armory NHS, a military museum housed in a brick arsenal built in 1847, traces the development of the rifle from pre-Revolutionary to modern times. The museum also displays a large collection of toy soldiers as well as the "Organ of Rifles," memorialized in a Longfellow poem. Other historic sites include the federal-style Alexander House, thought to have been built by architect Asher Benjamin, and the First Church, erected in 1819. Springfield is also the home of the Naismith Memorial Basketball Hall of Fame, dedicated to the game's American inventor. Write: Chamber of Commerce, Suite 600, 1500 Main St., Springfield 01115.

13 **Storrowton Village,** 1305 Memorial Ave., West Springfield 01089. A group of buildings dating from 1767 to 1834 have been reassembled around a village green. Costumed guides show visitors through homes, a schoolhouse, law office, blacksmith shop, meetinghouse, and tavern. Some buildings include craft demonstrations.

14 **Wayside Inn NHS,** Wayside Inn Road, South Sudbury 01776. Built at the close of the 17th century, this restored inn is among the oldest still in operation in the United States. Its present name derives from Longfellow's *Tales of a Wayside Inn.* The display rooms contain 18th-century furniture. On the grounds stand a chapel, schoolhouse, and reconstructed gristmill.

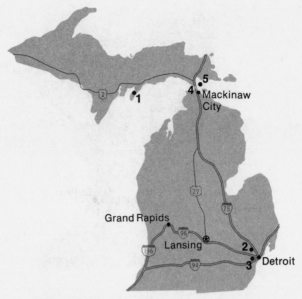

MICHIGAN

1 | **Fayette SP,** Garden 49835. Restoration has breathed new life into this ghost town, re-creating its iron-smelting heyday in the late 19th century. Among the restored buildings are homes with period furnishings, a doctor's office, opera house, and hotel. Charcoal and lime kilns have been rebuilt, and the old blast furnace partially restored to illustrate the principles of early iron smelting.

2 | **Franklin Village HD,** 32325 Franklin Rd., Franklin 48025. Franklin was founded in the 1820's as a rural community. Some 25 structures of historical or architectural interest are preserved within the town's historic district, including the Christopher Kline House (circa 1840), a wagon shop, mill, tavern, and the William Clemens House, once occupied by a cousin of Mark Twain.

3 | **Greenfield Village & Henry Ford Museum,** Dearborn 48121. Homes and workshops of inventors such as Thomas Edison, Henry Ford, and the Wright brothers have been assembled in a 260-acre "community" near Detroit to show how Americans lived and worked from pioneer days to the Industrial Revolution. See book, page 359.

4 | **Michilimackinac SP,** Box 873, Straits Ave., Mackinaw City 49701. This 27-acre park encompasses the site of Fort Michilimackinac, built by the French in 1715 to guard the straits between Lakes Huron and Michigan. Ten reconstructed buildings, surrounded by a log palisade, include a French church, storehouse, and barracks containing murals, dioramas, and interpretive exhibits. Visitors view cannon and musket demonstrations. A maritime museum displays the restored 1892 Old Mackinac Point Lighthouse.

5 | **Old Fort Mackinac,** Mackinac Island SP, Mackinac Island 49757. One of the nation's oldest forts, now a museum, was begun by the British in 1780. Occupied by the United States 16 years later, it served as a major military installation on the Great Lakes until 1895. Thick limestone ramparts surround 14 original buildings. Visitors examine blockhouses, officers' quarters, sally ports, even the "blackhole dungeon." Costumed guides conduct tours; uniformed "soldiers" fire cannons and muskets.

Nearby historic sites recall the days when fur trading thrived in the area. Among them are the original headquarters of the American Fur Company; Biddle House, built before 1800 and believed to be the oldest house on the island; the Benjamin Blacksmith Shop; Beaumont Memorial, a company store replica; and a replica of Fort Holmes, a log stronghold similar to the one used by the British during the War of 1812.

MINNESOTA

1 **Fort Snelling SP, NHL.** Completed in 1824, this stone fort on the Mississippi River oversaw affairs between settlers and Indians, and protected and regulated the American fur trade in the area. Its 15 original or reconstructed buildings include the Round Tower, believed to be the oldest structure in the state. Restoration of the fort continues. Exhibits and demonstrations show visitors the duties and activities of frontier soldiers and their families, from military drills to such crafts as blacksmithing, carpentry, and candle dipping. Write: Ft. Snelling History Center, St. Paul 55111.

2 **Grand Portage NM, NHL,** Box 666, Grand Marais 55604. During the 18th and early 19th centuries, voyageurs, traders, and trappers rendezvoused along this nine-mile trail from the western shore of Lake Superior to the navigable waters of the Pigeon River. From 1779 to 1803, Montreal's North West Company exchanged Eastern goods for Western furs at its "great depot" on the eastern end of the trail. The trading post, reconstructed and furnished to its 18th-century appearance, includes a stockade with gatehouse, kitchen, and a dining hall.

3 **Lumbertown, U.S.A.,** Box 387, Brainerd 56401. This village, a replica, takes visitors back to the 1870's, when lumbering towns prospered in Minnesota. Among some 30 buildings are a maple sugar plant, sawmill, furniture store, printshop, ice cream parlor, the Last Turn Saloon, a pioneer home, even an undertaker's parlor. Visitors ride a full-size replica of the first Northern Pacific train or cruise on the *Blueberry Bell* riverboat.

1 **Mendota.** This oldest permanent settlement in Minnesota served as a trading village for the American Fur Company in the 1820's and 1830's. A pioneer fur trader who became the state's first governor built the three-story, limestone Henry H. Sibley House in 1835. Thought to be Minnesota's first non-military stone house, it has been restored and refurbished with some original furniture. The restored 1836 home of pioneer Jean Baptiste Faribault also contains period furnishings and Indian artifacts. Write: Sibley House Association, Mendota 55050.

4 **Soudan Iron Mine,** Tower-Soudan HP, Soudan 55782. Within the 987-acre park, visitors explore the state's oldest and deepest iron mine, which operated from 1884 to 1962 and helped boost Minnesota to the nation's top iron producer. Ex-miner guides explain underground mining operations. The tour includes a 2,400-foot plunge in a mine elevator and an electric train ride through a 3,000-foot tunnel. The engine house, crusher building, drill shop, dryhouse, and open pits are also accessible.

MISSISSIPPI

1 | **Beauvoir**, Box 200, W. Beach Blvd., Biloxi 39531. Jefferson Davis, President of the Confederacy, spent the last 12 years of his life at this mansion, now fully restored and furnished with original Davis pieces. The 50-acre grounds include landscaped gardens and the cottage where Davis wrote *The Rise and Fall of the Confederate Government*.

2 | **Natchez.** Established by the French in 1716 and named for the Natchez Indians, ceded to England in 1763, captured by the Spanish in 1779, and finally made a part of the United States in 1798, Natchez enjoys a lively history. Buildings of note include nearly 100 antebellum mansions. Guidebooks are available for walking tours; many private homes are open during the month-long Spring Pilgrimage. Write: Chamber of Commerce, 716 Franklin St., Natchez 39120. See book, page 282.

3 | **Rosemont Plantation**, Woodville 39669. Roses planted by the mother of Confederate leader Jefferson Davis still bloom outside his boyhood home, a two-story "cottage" on a 270-acre plantation established by his father in 1810. The house, largely unchanged, is now being restored, along with outbuildings, orchards, gardens, and cotton fields. Furnishings in the house include an original whale-oil chandelier and Mrs. Davis's spinning wheel.

4 | **Vicksburg.** Its strategic location on the Mississippi River made this town a center of action during the Civil War—and a favorite site for today's Civil War buffs. Many antebellum structures have been restored. Cedar Grove, an elegant 17-room mansion on the riverbank, preserves a souvenir of bombardment from gunboats—a cannonball embedded in a parlor wall. McRaven House, a monument to changing architectural styles, was built as a frontier cottage in 1797, gained Louisiana Creole additions in 1836 and Greek Revival modifications in 1849. The Old Courthouse, built in 1858 and graced with tall, fluted columns and ornate iron grillwork, now houses a museum of antebellum and Confederate memorabilia. Write: Chamber of Commerce, Box 709, Vicksburg 39180.

4 | **Vicksburg NMP**, 3201 Clay St., Vicksburg 39180. Confederate forces and fortifications held strategic Vicksburg against attack after attack by Union armies, but the city finally fell July 4, 1863, after a 42-day siege. With victory the Union gained control of the entire Mississippi River, splitting the Confederacy and spelling doom for Southern hopes. Visitors follow a 16-mile tour road to battle sites, forts, trenches, and restored Shirley House, the only surviving wartime structure. The park's 1,700 acres also include Vicksburg National Cemetery, burial ground of 17,000 Union soldiers. See book, page 301.

MISSOURI

1 **Arrow Rock SHS,** Rte. 41, Arrow Rock 65320. This frontier town on the Missouri River was one of the starting points of the Santa Fe Trail. The town's 19th-century character comes to life at Arrow Rock Tavern, furnished in the style of Missouri pioneer times; a taproom has been converted into an 1840's general store. Visitors see the calaboose, a one-room stone jail said to have been used just once, and, according to the story, the prisoner raised such a ruckus that he was released. Other historic buildings at the site include the Old Court House, a gun shop, loom house, and several old homes.

2 **Fort Osage,** Box 122, Sibley 64088. The fort founded in 1808 by Gen. William Clark of the Lewis and Clark expedition has been restored. First U. S. Army post west of the Mississippi and first in the Louisiana Territory, Osage reigned as the most successful of the 28 "factories" (Indian trading posts) established by the government between 1795 and 1822 ostensibly to assure Indians fair prices for their furs. The factory contains rooms furnished from the early 1800's, when nearly all trappers, traders, and explorers stopped at this westernmost outpost in the territory.

3 **George Washington Carver NM,** Box 38, Diamond 64840. Carver was born into slavery on this small farm in 1860, and rose to become a distinguished teacher, botanist, and agronomist. The monument includes Carver's birthplace cabin site, a statue of the "Boy Carver," the Moses Carver House, and the family cemetery. A demonstration garden grows some of the crops he used in developing hundreds of useful by-products from peanuts, sweet potatoes, cotton, and soybeans.

4 **Harry S. Truman Library and Museum,** U. S. 24 and Delaware St., Independence 64050. A replica of Truman's White House office holds his personal and official papers, including the rough draft of his "Fair Deal" message to Congress, papers from the Potsdam Conference, and the 1945 Japanese surrender document, as well as the table on which, in 1945, the United Nations Charter was signed. The library contains books, films, and papers from his administration (1945-53), as well as items on loan from the National Archives, including President Wilson's 1917 declaration of war against Germany and President Roosevelt's 1941 "Day of Infamy" address. The courtyard grave site may be visited.

5 **Jefferson National Expansion NHS,** 11 N. Fourth St., St. Louis 63102. Situated on the original site of St. Louis, founded in 1764 by Pierre Laclède, the memorial commemorates the expansion of the United States after Thomas Jefferson's purchase of the Louisiana Territory in 1803. The stainless-steel Gateway Arch soars 630 feet above the mall. Visitors ride small cars inside the arch to an observation room at the top. An underground area houses the Museum of Western Expansion, which features exhibits of the 1800's. A visitor center movie theater shows films dramatizing the settlement of the West, the role of St. Louis in Western development, and the construction of the arch. The site also encompasses the Old Courthouse, scene of the Dred Scott trial, and the Old Cathedral, dedicated in 1834, one of the first built west of the Mississippi. See book, page 245.

6 **Mark Twain Boyhood Home and Museum,** 206-208 Hill St., Hannibal 63401. Samuel Clemens grew up in this two-story clapboard house. As Mark Twain, he later wrote *The Adventures of Huckleberry Finn* and *The Adventures of Tom Sawyer,* drawing on his boyhood experiences here. The restored house holds period furnishings and articles once owned by the author. The adjoining museum displays manuscripts, furniture, photographs, and other objects from Twain's life. A whitewashed fence recalls Tom Sawyer's famous chore. Across the street stands the Becky Thatcher house. Two miles south is Mark Twain Cave, inspiration for the cave in which Tom Sawyer and Becky Thatcher were lost.

7 **Pony Express Museum,** 914 Penn St., St. Joseph 64503. This brick building served as the eastern starting point for the Pony Express. In the year and a half before telegraph lines were completed in 1861, nearly 100 young men were engaged to ride the ten-day route reaching some 2,000 miles to Sacramento, California. The former stables now house a collection of photographs, drawings, saddles, weapons, and maps of express routes. Blacksmith and wheelwright shops have been restored.

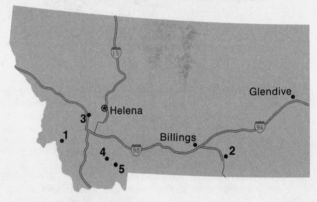

MONTANA

1 **Big Hole NB,** Box 237, Wisdom 59761. During the campaign to confine Indians to reservations, several bands of Nez Perce under Chief Joseph fled toward Canada. On August 9 and 10, 1877, they were attacked at Big Hole, but fought valiantly and escaped into Yellowstone country. Two self-guiding trails wind through the commemorative battlefield.

2 **Custer Battlefield NM,** Box 39, Crow Agency 59022. Commemorating the Battle of the Little Bighorn, this monument encompasses the ridge where Lt. Col. George Armstrong Custer made his "last stand," a secondary fighting area five miles south, a national cemetery, and a historical museum. See book, page 323.

3 **Grant Kohrs Ranch NHS,** Box 790, Deer Lodge 59722. Buildings of one of the nation's largest 19th-century ranches have been restored on the original site. The two-story, 1862 ranch house, at one time the largest home in Montana Territory, has been preserved intact, along with its original Victorian furniture and family records. Outbuildings include bunkhouses, stables, barns, buggy shed, blacksmith shop, granary, dairy, and the tack room. Demonstrations re-create chores and daily activities of ranchers a century ago. Livestock and 19th-century ranching equipment are on display. Visitors can take a self-guiding tour of buildings and grounds or accompany a Park Service guide.

4 Nevada City. A mining-camp suburb of Virginia City during the 1860's, Nevada City today preserves the spirit of its rough, rowdy past. Attractions include a nickelodeon collection, old-time fire engines, restored railroad cars, and a restored 1860's stage station. Visitors can ride the Alder Gulch Short Line work train. Write: Bovey Restorations, Box 338, Virginia City 59755.

5 Virginia City HD. When prospectors struck gold at Alder Gulch in 1863, Virginia City overnight became a roaring town notorious for lawlessness. Claim jumpers, vigilantes, and road agents (secretly led by the town sheriff) dueled with wits and fists and guns. Refurbished false-front buildings line Main Street: assay office, general store, blacksmith shop, saloon, hotel, Wells Fargo office. The Opera House, a converted livery stable, stages 19th-century melodramas nightly during the summer. Write: Bovey Restorations, Box 338, Virginia City 59755.

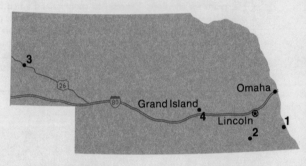

NEBRASKA

1 Brownville HD, Brownville 68321. Restoration continues on what was once a bustling frontier town and trading center on the Missouri River during the steamboat era. Visitors tour the Brownville Museum, displaying antiques in the Victorian home of a riverboat captain; the Carson House, with furnishings from the mid-1800's; the Muir House, containing Victorian furniture, clothing, and household items; and the Lone Tree Saloon, one of the 13 that stood in this town—and Jesse James's favorite. The saloon, once the opera house, is now a working mill.

2 Homestead NM, RFD 3, Beatrice 68310. Daniel Freeman, one of the first to file for free land under the Homestead Act of 1862, chose this spot to stake his claim. The act entitled each applicant to 160 acres, which became his after he occupied and cultivated the claim for five years. The monument includes a trail through the tall-grass prairie, the graves of Freeman and his wife, and a display of pioneer tools and furniture. An 1867 timbered cabin, moved here from a neighboring farm, has been restored as a typical homestead dwelling.

3 Scotts Bluff NM, Box 427, Gering 69341. Landmark of the journey west on the Oregon Trail, this 700-foot-high promontory was a welcome sight for pioneers, traders, and gold seekers. A museum tells the story of westward migration and exhibits tools and vehicles of the period. See book, page 246.

4 Stuhr Museum of the Prairie Pioneer, Jct. of Rtes. 34 and 281, Grand Island 68801. Some 55 buildings from surrounding towns form a typical prairie town. Main Street is lined with a bank, barbershop, general store, hotel, houses, post office, blacksmith shop, and barns. A vintage steam train makes scheduled runs over tracks that lead to an old depot. A museum outside town houses relics of Nebraska's early days.

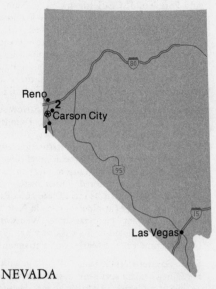

NEVADA

1 **Mormon Station SHM.** This site at Genoa commemorates Nevada's first permanent settlement, established by traders dispatched by Brigham Young in 1850. The station grew into a stopping point for travelers on the Humboldt section of the California Trail, and in 1851 became the site of the first attempt at Nevada territorial government. Today visitors wander through a log replica of the trading post and stockade, and a museum in the old county courthouse. Write: Nevada State Parks, 201 South Fall St., Carson City 89710.

2 **Virginia City HD.** Nevada's largest mining town has been restored to its 1870's appearance, recapturing its heyday as "Queen of the Comstock Lode" and home of bonanza kings, adventurers, and rogues from all over the world. Write: Storey County Chamber of Commerce, Box 464, Virginia City 89440. See book, page 333.

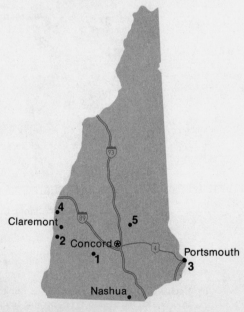

NEW HAMPSHIRE

1 **Franklin Pierce Homestead NHL,** Hillsboro 03244. Franklin Pierce, 14th President (1853-57), lived here for the first 30 years of his life. The federal-style house was built in 1804 by Pierce's father, Benjamin, who served twice as governor of New Hampshire.

2 | **Old Fort No. 4,** Charlestown 03603. Named for a land grant called Township No. 4, this log fort, begun in 1746, was successfully defended three years later by a handful of settlers against a large force of French and Indians. In 1777 Gen. John Stark assembled his troops here before their victorious battle at Bennington, Vermont. Exhibits include reconstructions of the Great Hall, a watchtower, stockade, barns, and other buildings.

3 | **Portsmouth.** Fine old houses along narrow streets retain the flavor of colonial seafaring days. Founded in 1630, Portsmouth was first called Strawbery Banke. This name has been given to the historic restoration project on the Piscataqua riverfront where the original colonists settled. Nearly 40 buildings dating from 1695 to the early 19th century have been restored. Other historic Portsmouth buildings open to visitors include the 1664 Richard Jackson House, one of the oldest houses in New Hampshire, and the elegant Georgian-style Wentworth-Gardner House (1760), noted for its woodcarving. Write: Chamber of Commerce, 500 Market St., Portsmouth 03801.

4 | **Saint-Gaudens NHS.** Famed American sculptor Augustus Saint-Gaudens spent his most productive years in this 18th-century house, originally an inn. He supervised extensive remodeling, added studios, and installed formal gardens. More than half his work is on permanent exhibit. The 150-acre site, located in Cornish, includes woodlands with self-guiding trails. Sunday concerts are held during the summer months. Write: Superintendent, Box 73, Cornish 03745.

5 | **Shaker Village, Inc.,** Canterbury 03224. This Shaker community, founded in 1792, lies 14 miles north of Concord. The original meetinghouse has been turned into a museum of Shaker inventions, industries, and simple furniture. Other restored frame buildings open to visitors include a sister's shop, schoolhouse, and carriage house, all dating from the early 19th century.

NEW JERSEY

1 | **Batsto HS,** Rte. 542, Hammonton 08037. The Batsto Iron Works, founded in 1766, became an important iron-making center and a major supplier of munitions for the American army during the Revolutionary War and the War of 1812. After the iron furnaces shut down in 1848, the community continued to produce window glass until 1867. Restored Batsto Village features a 36-room Victorian ironmaster's mansion, sawmill, workers' cottages, blacksmith and wheelwright shops, gristmill, general store displaying period pieces, and the oldest known operating post office in the nation.

2   **Edison NHS,** Main St. and Lakeside Ave., West Orange 07052. Thomas Alva Edison developed many of his inventions and scientific ideas at the laboratory he built in 1887. On display are Edison's library, his chemical lab, machine shop, and inventions that include the first tinfoil phonograph, early incandescent lamps, and a reconstruction of the first motion picture studio. A mile away stands Glenmont, Edison's 23-room Victorian home, furnished almost entirely with pieces owned by the inventor when he lived here from 1886 until his death in 1931. Edison and his second wife, Mina, are buried behind the house.

3   **Grover Cleveland Birthplace,** 207 Bloomfield Ave., Caldwell 07006. Grover Cleveland, the only New Jersey native elected President (1885-89 and 1893-97), was born in this three-story frame house in 1837. Visitors see Cleveland mementos, including his wooden cradle.

4   **Historic Towne of Smithville,** U. S. 9, Smithville 08201. Buildings typical of the early 1800's re-create a southern New Jersey crossroads community. Clustered around the Smithville Inn, a former stagecoach stop now run as a restaurant, are a sweet shop, general store, winery, wood carving factory, and bakery. Some shops sell 19th-century wares; others display Early American arts and crafts. On the town pond floats a "bugeye"—a 19th-century oyster boat from Chesapeake Bay.

5   **Howell Iron Works,** Allaire SP, Rte. 524, Allaire 07727. For 26 years this bog ore furnace and forge turned out iron cookware. Founded in 1822 by James Allaire, the furnace produced air chambers for Robert Fulton's steamboat *Clermont* and pipes for New York City's first waterworks. Allaire created a model community for his 500 employees: 60 comfortable homes, a school, company store, and stagecoach line. The community church, enameling furnace, bakery, manager's cottage, carriage house, store, blacksmith and carpenter's shop, and houses appear as they did during Allaire's heyday.

6   **Morristown NHP,** Morristown 07960. General Washington and his weary army endured sickness, starvation, and mutiny in this small village, only 30 miles from British-held New York City. George and Martha Washington spent the bitter winter of 1779-80 in the Ford Mansion, now furnished with period pieces. A museum behind the house offers films and exhibits on 19th-century artifacts and weapons. Fort Nonsense, now an overlook, was purportedly built to keep the troops busy. Soldiers camped three miles away at Jockey Hollow, site of reconstructed log huts and a camp hospital. The Wick House, a New England-style farmhouse, served as the headquarters of American Maj. Gen. Arthur St. Clair.

7   **Trenton.** At various times during the Revolutionary War, British, Hessian, and Continental soldiers and loyalist refugees quartered in the Old Barracks, erected in 1758-59 to billet English troops. George Washington memorabilia and colonial antiques adorn the stone barracks. Washington and Lafayette stayed at the Trent House, oldest in the city, built in 1719 by New Jersey's first chief justice. The Trenton Battle Monument commemorates the American victory at the Battle of Trenton. Write: Mercer County Chamber of Commerce, 240 West State St., Trenton 08608.

8   **Waterloo Village Restoration,** Rte. 206, near Netcong 07857. Known as Andover Forge during the Revolution, this town furnished the Continental army with musket barrels and cannonballs. Once a bustling village on the Morris Canal, Waterloo is now a cluster of restored Early American buildings dating to 1760. Visitors explore the stagecoach inn, gristmill, church, apothecary, general store, smithy, carriage house, and craft shops.

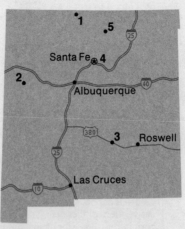

NEW MEXICO

1   **Cumbres & Toltec Scenic Railroad,** Box 789, Chama 87520. Summer sightseeing trips are offered on this 64-mile narrow-gauge line between Chama and Antonito, Colorado. Remnant of a once-important section of the Denver & Rio Grande, the line still operates as it did in 1925. A coal-burning locomotive draws boxcars rebuilt for passengers along a scenic route over high bridges, through tunnels, across the spectacular Toltec Gorge, and over 10,015-foot Cumbres Pass.

2   **El Morro NM,** Ramah 87321. The sandstone face of 200-foot-high Inscription Rock, called El Morro ("the headland" or "the bluff") by the Spanish, has provided a surface for graffiti over the ages. Ancient Indian petroglyphs are jumbled among inscriptions by explorers, soldiers, and settlers. In one, Don Juan de Oñate, colonizer and governor of New Mexico, records his presence in 1605. Ruins of two Indian pueblos may be visited on top of the bluff. See book, page 23.

3   **Lincoln County Courthouse SHM,** Box 36, Lincoln 88338. This two-story adobe building held the jail from which the notorious outlaw Billy the Kid escaped in 1881 after killing two guards. Exhibits in the restored courthouse depict frontier history. An annual Billy the Kid pageant, held in August, features a folk play, fiddlers' contest, parade, and Pony Express race.

4   **Santa Fe.** Founded in 1610 as the Spanish capital of New Mexico, Santa Fe is the oldest seat of government in the United States. The Palace of the Governors NHL stands in the historic central plaza, which also marks the southern end of the Santa Fe Trail. Santa Fe's religious heritage lives on in Cristo Rey Church, the largest adobe building in the nation; imposing St. Francis Cathedral; Our Lady of Light Chapel, with its intriguing spiral stairway; and the San Miguel Mission, one of the nation's oldest churches. Ten miles southeast of Santa Fe lies Glorieta Pass Battlefield, where Union troops in 1862 repelled a Confederate invasion of New Mexico. Write: Chamber of Commerce, Box 1928, Santa Fe 87504. See book, page 230.

5   **Taos.** Settled by the Spanish in 1615, the city reflects a blend of Spanish and Indian cultures in the midst of magnificent scenery. Frontiersman Kit Carson is honored by the Carson House NHL, where he lived for 25 years. He is buried nearby in Kit Carson SMem. At nearby Taos Pueblo NHL more than 500 Indian families live in two five-storied adobe communal dwellings little different from those the Spanish saw in 1540. Ceremonial dances and fiestas are held here. Ranchos de Taos, four miles south of town, boasts the Mission of St. Francis of Assisi, one of the Southwest's finest 18th-century churches. The ornamental wooden altar backdrop is believed to date from the church's founding. Write: Chamber of Commerce, Drawer I, Taos 87571. See book, page 230.

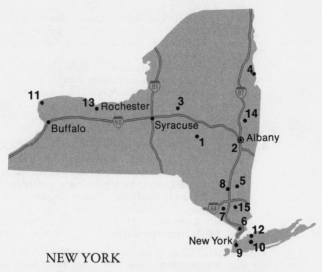

NEW YORK

1   **Cooperstown.** Founded in 1786 by the father of novelist James Fenimore Cooper, Cooperstown is where Abner Doubleday purportedly devised modern baseball in 1839. The National Baseball Hall of Fame and Museum enshrines the bats, gloves, and belongings of immortalized players. The Farmer's Museum and Village Crossroads exhibits Early American farming, household, and craft implements. A printshop, pharmacy, doctor's and lawyer's offices, and other relocated buildings form a rural village. The imposing Fenimore House displays James Fenimore Cooper manuscripts and mementos. Write: Chamber of Commerce, Box 46, Cooperstown 13326.

2   **Dutch Homes on the Hudson.** Houses of early Dutch settlers and their descendants dot the Hudson River Valley. Write: Division of Tourism, 1 Commerce Plaza, Albany 12245. See book, page 41.

2   **Erie Canal.** Mules and horses towed wooden barges along the 363-mile-long "ditch" that linked Albany with Buffalo. Inaugurated in 1825 at the then-astonishing cost of $7,143,789, "Clinton's Folly" speeded trade and settlement of the Old Northwest. Original locks can be seen at Fort Hunter, west of Amsterdam, and at Lockport. Along the canal, near Rome, is the Oriskany Battlefield, scene of a Revolutionary War battle. Write: Dept. of Transportation, 1220 Washington Ave., Albany 12232.

3   **Fort Stanwix NM,** 112 E. Park St., Rome 13440. Brig. Gen. John Stanwix directed construction of this star-shaped fort in 1758 on a site overlooking an important portage on the Mohawk River. In 1777 an American garrison warded off a British invasion from Canada. The reconstructed fort displays a storehouse, bombproof, barracks, and casemates. Exhibits at the Fort Stanwix Museum depict the history of the upper Mohawk Valley.

4   **Fort Ticonderoga,** Rte. 74, Ticonderoga 12883. In 1755 the French leveled a mountaintop to build star-shaped Fort Carillon, a strategic outpost on Lake Champlain. Scene of struggles between the French and English, who captured and renamed it Ticonderoga in 1759, the fort fell to Ethan Allen's Green Mountain Boys during the Revolution. Reconstructed according to original French plans, the stronghold includes a parade ground, bastions, barracks, and ramparts. A well-marked battlefield girds the fort, and a museum houses an outstanding collection of uniforms, weapons, artifacts, documents, and paintings.

5   **Hyde Park** 12538. Franklin D. Roosevelt Home NHS, birthplace of the 32nd President, served as the summer White House from 1933 until 1945. A self-guided tour takes visitors through the rambling 35-room house. The icehouse and stables may be seen, as well as the rose garden where Franklin and Eleanor are buried. The Franklin

D. Roosevelt Library and Museum contains papers, books, letters, and mementos from the Roosevelt era, including ship models, gifts from world leaders, naval prints and paintings.

Majestic trees flank the driveway leading to Vanderbilt Mansion, a 54-room, 14-bath palace built in 1896-98 for financier Frederick W. Vanderbilt. His "royal palace" contains art treasures, antiques, and lavish furnishings. Visitors strolling the 212-acre estate view a coach house, Italian gardens, and 150-year-old exotic trees.

6 **Lyndhurst,** 635 S. Broadway, Tarrytown 10591. Original furnishings, paintings, statuary, and bric-a-brac in this Gothic Revival mansion, once the home of railroad tycoon Jay Gould, reflect the lavish life-styles of the Gilded Age. Carved woodwork, marble fireplaces, and stained-glass windows adorn the rooms. Other buildings on the 67-acre estate include a 400-foot-long greenhouse, Gothic-style gardener's cottage, and an 1865 coach house.

7 **Museum Village in Orange County,** Museum Village Rd., Monroe 10950. Tools and objects in 30 buildings portray the era of homespun, craft shop, and emerging industry. Radiating from the village green are a dress emporium, wagonmaker's shop, apothecary, weaver's shop, stone schoolhouse, cider mill and scale house, cobbler's shop. Daily craft demonstrations include broommaking, weaving, printing, blacksmithing, and pottery making.

8 **New Paltz.** Charming stone houses and quaint streets attract visitors to New Paltz, founded in 1692 by a dozen French Huguenots. Tours of several stone houses still standing on one of America's oldest streets begin at the Deyo Hall. Nearby are the Terwilliger House, an 18th-century stone dwelling, and Locust Lawn, a federal-style mansion. Write: Huguenot Historical Society, Box 339, New Paltz 12561.

9 **New York City.**

Manhattan. Amid the canyons of the modern city, a few historical buildings remain. Jutting bowsprits shadow the South Street Seaport Museum, a seven-block restoration of New York's first shipping center along the East River. At the South Street docks, visitors clamber aboard ships from the age of sail and steam—the square-rigger *Wavertree,* the four-masted bark *Peking,* the *Ambrose* lightship. Restored shops and countinghouses of the once-teeming 19th-century neighborhood contain model-ship galleries, a ship museum, book and chart shop, stationers and printing museum, and marine art gallery. Pungent aromas waft on the salt air from the Fulton Fish Market, in continuous operation since 1821.

At nearby Fraunces Tavern, now a restaurant and Revolutionary War museum, George Washington bade farewell to his troops. The first President worshiped at St. Paul's Chapel (1766), oldest church in Manhattan. Castle Clinton NM in Battery Park, built in 1811 to defend New York Harbor, saw service successively as a promenade and entertainment center, an immigration depot, and the New York aquarium; it is now restored as a fort. Theodore Roosevelt Birthplace NHS, the brownstone boyhood home of the only President born in New York City, contains Victorian furnishings and family memorabilia.

Farther uptown, Hamilton Grange, the country estate of Alexander Hamilton, houses belongings of the first Secretary of the Treasury. Washington directed the Battle of Harlem Heights from the Morris-Jumel Mansion, a brick dwelling furnished with federal and empire pieces.

Liberty Island. Designed by Frédéric Auguste Bartholdi, the Statue of Liberty commemorates America's alliance with France during the Revolution. At the statue's base stands the American Museum of Immigration.

Staten Island. Colonial furnishings decorate the Conference House, scene of an abortive peace conference to stave off the Revolution. Fort Wadsworth, oldest continually manned military installation in the country, defended

New York Harbor during the War of 1812 as well as World Wars I and II. The ongoing Richmondtown Restoration will encompass 40 buildings that reflect the evolution of an American village from the 17th to 19th centuries. The project now includes the Voorlezer's House, one of the oldest schoolhouses in the country; Lake-Tysen House, a furnished Dutch colonial farmhouse; Old County Clerk's and Surrogate's Office, now a museum; Treasure House, named for the discovery in its walls of $7,000 in gold coins, probably hidden there during the Revolution by a British paymaster.

Write: New York City Convention and Visitors Bureau, 2 Columbus Circle, New York 10019; Staten Island Chamber of Commerce, 130 Bay St., Staten Island 10301.

10 | **Old Bethpage Village Restoration**, Round Swamp Rd., Old Bethpage 11804. A rural village typical of the first half of the 19th century comes alive at Old Bethpage. Buildings moved here from various parts of Long Island include a smithy, carpenter's shop, tavern, church, stores, and houses. A working farm illustrates agricultural life, crops, and methods of the mid-1800's.

11 | **Old Fort Niagara**, Rte. 18F, near Youngstown 14174. During the summer, 18th-century military drills and pageantry regale visitors to this French-built stone fortress. Fortifications include cannons, artillery tunnels, moat, drawbridge, powder magazine, blockhouse, and hot shot furnace. The only French-fortified castle (1726) in the nation features a gun deck, prison, and Jesuit chapel.

12 | **Oyster Bay.** African masks, animal skins, hunting trophies, and other Theodore Roosevelt memorabilia festoon Sagamore Hill, the 22-room Victorian "cottage" that served as the summer White House from 1901 to 1909. The Old Orchard Museum, Georgian home of Theodore Roosevelt, Jr., exhibits items about the family life and career of his father. At Raynham Hall, British headquarters during the Revolution, the conspiracy between Maj. John André and Benedict Arnold to betray West Point was in large part exposed. Write: Oyster Bay Historical Society, 20 Summit St., Oyster Bay 11771.

13 | **Rochester.** Dwellings range from the Stone-Tolan House, a restored pioneer farmstead, to handsome Greek Revival mansions—Woodside and Campbell-Whittlesey House. Displays in the Susan B. Anthony House NHL, home of a leading suffragette, chronicle the ratification of the Nineteenth Amendment. The home of George Eastman, "father of American photography," contains a museum that traces the history of photography and cinematography. A score of buildings at the Genesee Country Museum in nearby Mumford re-create an early 19th-century village. Write: Chamber of Commerce, 55 St. Paul St., Rochester 14604.

14 | **Saratoga NHP**, U. S. 4, Stillwater 12170. This 2,700-acre park commemorates the defeat of the British by colonial forces in 1777. Called "the turning point of the American Revolution," the battles sparked colonial militia enlistments and encouraged France to aid America. An auto-and-walking tour of the battlefield includes the American and British headquarters and a log cabin similar to those used by British and colonial troops. See book, page 140.

15 | **United States Military Academy**, West Point 10996. Militarily important since Revolutionary days, the Point commands a strategic position on the Hudson River. In 1780 Benedict Arnold, then commander of the post, made an unsuccessful attempt to deliver West Point to the British. Earlier in the war the Americans strung a huge chain across the river to block British ships. Some links are displayed near Battle Monument, dedicated to soldiers killed during the Civil War. Exhibits at the West Point Museum trace the history of the Academy, established by Congress in 1802 to train army officers. See book, page 134.

NORTH CAROLINA

1 | **Bath SHS.** North Carolina's oldest incorporated town, Bath was founded in 1705 as the colony's port of entry and seat of government—and also served briefly as Blackbeard's hideaway. The silver candelabra of St. Thomas Church were a gift from King George II; its bell was presented by Queen Anne. The restored Palmer-Marsh House (1744) and Bonner House (1825) are furnished with period antiques. A visitor center offers tours of the town. Write: Historic Bath, Bath 27808.

2 | **Bentonville Battleground SHS,** Newton Grove 28366. The largest Civil War land action in the state—and the last attempt to stop Sherman's army from joining Grant's in Virginia—raged here for three days in March 1865. Confederate General Johnston's 30,000 men were no match for Sherman's 60,000; Johnston finally withdrew. The 6,000-acre preserve includes a museum, a Confederate cemetery, and restored Harper House, a residence used at various times by both sides as a field hospital.

3 | **Biltmore Estate NHL,** Box 5375, Asheville 28803. George W. Vanderbilt built this French Renaissance mansion in the late 1800's. See book, page 371.

4 | **Carl Sandburg Home NHS,** Box 395, Flat Rock 28731. At this secluded 247-acre mountain farm, Sandburg spent the last 22 years of his life before his death in 1967. Here he wrote his only novel, several volumes of history and poetry, and his autobiography. Visitors tour the restored main house, built in 1838, inspect the numerous farm buildings, and wander woods and pastures.

5 | **Edenton HD.** This town on Queen Anne's Creek was incorporated in 1712 and finally named in 1722 in honor of Governor Charles Eden. It served as unofficial capital of the colony for 40 years. Almost 50 historic sites are preserved, some built in the 1720's. The Georgian-style Chowan County Courthouse (1767) is the oldest in use in the state. The nearby Teapot Memorial—a bronze teapot—commemorates the "Edenton Tea Party" on October 25, 1774, when 51 women gathered on the courthouse green to forswear the drinking of tea or the wearing of any English "manufacture." Write: Chamber of Commerce, 116 E. King St., Edenton 27932.

6 | **Fort Raleigh NHS,** Rte. 1, Box 675, Manteo 27954. From 1585 to 1590 Sir Walter Raleigh attempted—and failed—to settle the first English colonies in "Virginia" at this Roanoke Island site. The disappearance of the last colony remains unexplained to this day. Exhibits tell the story of these colonies. A granite memorial honors Virginia Dare, first English child born in the New World. Visitors explore reconstructed Fort Raleigh, stroll a woodland nature trail, and enjoy a symphonic drama, "Lost Colony," presented during the summer. See book, page 29.

7 | **Guilford Courthouse NMP,** Box 9806, Greensboro 27429. Lord Cornwallis's redcoats won the battle here on March 15, 1781, against Gen. Nathanael Green's inexperienced militia, but the British suffered such heavy losses that they were unable to carry the offensive farther. Markers, monuments, a film, and exhibits explain the battle that set the stage for Cornwallis's surrender at Yorktown, Virginia, seven months later.

8 James K. Polk Birthplace SHS, U.S. 521, Pineville 28134. The 11th President (1845-49), born here in 1795, lived on this farm until the family moved to Tennessee in 1806. The log cabin and farm buildings have been reconstructed. A museum displays exhibits on Polk's career.

9 Moores Creek NB, Box 69, Currie 28435. Tories and patriots clashed in a brief but crucial battle here early in 1776. The patriot rout of the larger British forces, which included a battalion of Highland Scots, prevented a rendezvous with British ships on the coast, proved the strength of the patriots, and helped form North Carolina's decision to vote for independence—the first such vote among the colonies. A walking tour of the battlefield passes earthworks and monuments—one honoring the heroic women who aided in the victory, especially Mary Slocum, who supposedly rode 65 miles to help the wounded.

10 Oconaluftee Indian Village, Cherokee 28719. Located on the Cherokee Reservation bordering Great Smoky Mountains NP, this village re-creates Indian life as it was 200 years ago. Cherokees in traditional costume work at such skills as woodcarving, basketry, beadwork, and arrow- and dart-making. At the nearby Museum of the Cherokee Indian, artifacts and exhibits document the culture and history of the Cherokee nation. During summer, an outdoor drama, "Unto These Hills," tells the story of the tribe's removal from their lands in 1838.

11 Old Salem, Winston-Salem 27108. The Moravian community here has been restored to its 18th-century appearance. See book, page 122.

12 Tryon Palace Restoration Complex, 610 Pollock St., New Bern 28560, includes the 18th-century Governor's Palace and the state's first capitol. See book, page 120.

6 Wright Brothers NMem, Kill Devil Hills. Full-scale reproductions of the 1902 glider and 1903 flying machine made and flown by Wilbur and Orville Wright are displayed. Nearby stand the 60-foot Wright Memorial Shaft and a reconstruction of their work sheds. Markers measure the flights made on December 17, 1903, over these Outer Banks dunes. Write: Superintendent, Rte. 1, Box 675, Manteo 27957. See book, page 366.

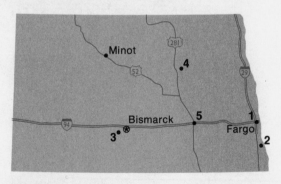

NORTH DAKOTA

1 Bonanzaville, U.S.A., I-94 and U.S. 10, West Fargo 58078. Some 45 buildings reconstruct a pioneer village typical of the Red River Valley's bonanza agricultural era of the 1870's, when land was sold in huge tracts and a thousand men might work one farm. Among the attractions are the town hall with its two-cell jail; a livery stable with buggies and carriages; a train depot with locomotive, passenger cars, and caboose; barbershop; theater; printshop; blacksmith shop; and other buildings. A museum contains additional old-time displays and relics.

2 Fort Abercrombie SHS, Abercrombie 58001. The first federal fort in what is now North Dakota was established in 1858 to protect wagon trains and traffic on the Red

River of the North. Sioux Indians attacked the fort twice during the 1862 Minnesota Uprising and once kept it under siege for more than a month. Abandoned in 1877, the fort today includes the original guardhouse, reconstructed blockhouses and stockade, and a museum containing military, pioneer, and Indian exhibits.

3 **Fort Abraham Lincoln SP**, Rte. 1806, Mandan 58554. The 975-acre park includes reconstructed portions of an Indian village and federal fort, and a museum that tells the story of both. Fort McKeen, built in 1872 to protect engineers and workers of the Northern Pacific Railroad, was renamed for Abraham Lincoln the following year and enlarged to accommodate Lt. Col. George Armstrong Custer's 7th Cavalry. From Fort Lincoln, Custer led his men to their historic "last stand" against a large Indian force at the Battle of the Little Bighorn in 1876.

4 **Fort Totten SHS**, Rte. 57, fifteen miles southwest of Devils Lake 58301. Built between 1867 and 1872 to protect the overland stage route from southern Minnesota to western Montana, Fort Totten remains one of the best-preserved relics from the era of the Plains Indian wars. Now located on the Devils Lake Sioux Indian Reservation, the fort contains 16 of its original brick buildings surrounding the old parade ground, plus a pioneer museum, old-time general store, and a wildlife exhibit. A summer theater stages musical productions.

5 **Frontier Village**, Rte. I-94, Jamestown 58401. Several buildings moved to this site re-create pioneer life on the Dakota prairies. The village includes a frame church, log cabin, drugstore, printshop, schoolhouse, railroad depot with restored caboose, land office, jail, art exhibits, and a large statue of a bison commemorating the great herds that once roamed the grasslands.

OHIO

1 **Adena SMem**, Adena Rd., Chillicothe 45601. In the first capital of Ohio, the state's sixth governor erected this stately stone mansion in 1807. The house is furnished with period antiques. A tenant house, wash house, barn, and springhouse have been reconstructed on original sites.

2 **Au Glaize Village**, Krouse Rd., near Defiance 43512. A rural community of the late 1800's comes to life as visitors tour a cider mill, railroad station, doctor's office, log cabin, post office, lockkeeper's house, schoolhouse, blacksmith shop, and farm museums.

3 **Campus Martius SMem Museum**, 601 Second St., Marietta 45750. The settlers who founded Marietta, oldest community in Ohio, lived in a fortified village known as Campus Martius ("Field of Mars"), now the site of a pioneer museum. On display are relics associated with Ohio's early years as well as the restored frame house of Rufus Putnam, leader of the group that settled here in 1788. One wing contains the Ohio River Museum, devoted to the steamboat era. The one-room Ohio Company Land Office, moved from its original site, served as the first office building in the Northwest Territory.

4 Cincinnati. Birthplace of the only man to serve as President (1909-13) as well as Chief Justice, the William Howard Taft NHS has been restored with family belongings and period furnishings. The stern-wheeler *Delta Queen,* launched in 1926, plies the Mississippi and Ohio Rivers, stopping at historic towns and plantations. Write: Chamber of Commerce, 120 W. Fifth St., Cincinnati 45202.

5 Geauga County Historical Society Century Village, Box 153, Burton 44021. A rural community assembled around the village green captures the flavor of life in the 1850's and 1860's, when Connecticut claimed northeastern Ohio as its Western Reserve. The buildings, more than a century old, include New England-style houses, a church, railroad depot, ladies' dress and hat shop, general store, farm complex, and cabinet shop.

6 Hale Farm and Western Reserve Village, 2686 Oak Hill Rd., Bath 44210. This museum village evokes the days when New England pioneers poured into the Western Reserve. The enclave centers around the 1826 federal-style brick home of Jonathan Hale, a farmer who moved here from Connecticut. Other buildings on the village green hark back to frontier life between 1825 and 1850. Artisans demonstrate pioneer crafts.

7 Harding Home and Museum, 380 Mount Vernon Ave., Marion 43302. From this Victorian frame house, Warren G. Harding conducted the "Front Porch Campaign" that led to his election as 29th President (1921-23). Original furnishings, wallpaper, and gaslight fixtures adorn the home where Harding spent much of his adult life. A museum behind the house displays Harding memorabilia.

8 Lawnfield, 8095 Mentor Ave., Mentor 44060. Family belongings, furnishings, and a memorial library decorate the rambling clapboard Victorian mansion of James A. Garfield, 20th President (1881). Also on the grounds are his campaign office, barn, carriage house, caretaker's cottage, and windmill-pumphouse.

9 Roscoe Village, 381 Hill St., Coshocton 43812. Founded in 1816, Roscoe flourished as a grain-shipping port on the Ohio and Erie Canal until the railroad came in the late 19th century. Several restored buildings, including the 1836 Johnson-Williams House, mirror life during Roscoe's heyday. A horse-drawn barge nearby shuttles visitors along a remnant of the canal during the summer months.

10 Rutherford B. Hayes SMem, 1337 Hayes Ave., Fremont 43420. General, congressman, governor of Ohio, and 19th President (1877-81), Hayes moved to this wooded 25-acre estate, Spiegel Grove, in 1873. The extensive Presidential library houses Hayes' books, papers, letters, and diaries. The museum displays family mementos, including White House china and a Presidential carriage. A granite monument marks the tomb of Hayes and his wife.

11 Schoenbrunn Village SMem, off U.S. 250, New Philadelphia 44663. In 1772 Moravians founded a mission to the Indians here and erected 60 log cabins as well as the first school and church in the state. Today a museum and the rebuilt church, school, and log dwellings reflect pioneer life in Schoenbrunn. Each summer, costumed guides demonstrate cooking, sewing, candlemaking, mat weaving, chinking, fence wattling, and field work.

12 Zoar Village SMem, Rte. 212, Zoar 44697. Restored homes, gardens, and shops depict life in Zoar, established as a virtually self-sustaining communal society in 1817 by members of a German pietist sect. See book, page 225.

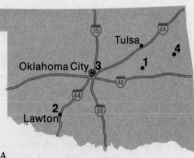

OKLAHOMA

1 | **Creek National Capitol NHL,** Town Square, Okmulgee 74447. Forced to leave their Georgia and Alabama homelands, the Creek Indians settled around Okmulgee in 1836. Some 40 years later, they remodeled their form of representative government along federal lines, with a constitution and this capitol building. It holds chambers for two governmental bodies, the House of Kings and the House of Warriors. Displays include Indian crafts, clothes, and weapons.

2 | **Fort Sill,** Fort Sill 73503. Established by Gen. Phil Sheridan in 1869, this military post for two decades helped control the Indians of the southern plains. The many stone buildings still standing include the old guardhouse where the Apache chieftain Geronimo was imprisoned. He settled as a farmer at the fort and was buried in the post's Apache cemetery, often called "the Indian Arlington" because of the many chiefs interred there. Other structures include an 1870 stone corral containing army and pioneer horse-drawn vehicles, blacksmith tools, and Indian tepees; and the 1875 post chapel.

3 | **National Cowboy Hall of Fame,** 1700 N.E. 63rd St., Oklahoma City 73111. This center commemorates the men and women who contributed to the development of the West. Among its attractions: paintings, life-size dioramas, and statues such as James Earl Fraser's *End of the Trail;* the "West of Yesterday" recalling Indian and pioneer villages through sight and sound; a stagecoach, sod house, gun shop, and cowboy chuck wagon.

4 | **Tahlequah,** Box 419, 74464. The Cherokee government's supreme court, capitol, and national prison still stand in this capital city of the Cherokee Indian nation. The lavish Murrell Home was built in 1845 by a prominent Virginia merchant who endured the trip over the Trail of Tears with the Cherokees. Tsa-La-Gi re-creates an early Cherokee Indian village. During summer months, "Trail of Tears," an outdoor dramatization, recounts the tragic struggle of the Cherokee nation between 1838 and 1907.

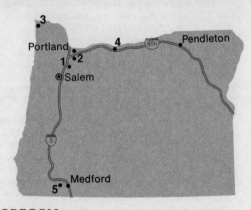

OREGON

1 | **Aurora Colony Historical Society Bldgs.,** Box 202, Second and Liberty Sts., Aurora 97002. Established in the 1850's by devout German pioneers under the leadership of

Dr. William Keil, the Aurora Colony dedicated itself to a communal ideal. For more than 30 years it prospered, holding miles of fertile farmland in common ownership and producing for the common good. Visitors tour the 1864 Kraus House, a family dwelling with handmade furnishings typical of the group's skillful craftsmanship; the Ox Barn Museum, filled with handmade tools, utensils, musical instruments, and other relics; and the austere Steinbach Cabin, one of Aurora Colony's first log homes.

2 **Dr. John McLoughlin House NHS,** 713 Center St., Oregon City 97045. As chief factor of the Hudson's Bay Company Columbia Department. Dr. McLoughlin prevented many conflicts with local Indians, expanded fur trading, and helped settlers start farms in the Oregon country. Built in 1845-46, the colonial-style building is furnished with family pieces and period articles.

3 **Fort Clatsop NMem,** Box 604-FC, Astoria 97103. This historical reconstruction of Lewis and Clark's 1805-06 winter headquarters includes costumed demonstrations and interpretive displays. See book, page 199.

4 **Fort Dalles Surgeon's Quarters,** Box 806, The Dalles 97058. This 1856 Gothic cottage is all that remains of old Fort Dalles, a frontier outpost and base of military operations against Indians from 1856 to 1859. The building now houses a museum of frontier relics, including a collection of military weapons. Old stagecoaches and covered wagons are exhibited in nearby sheds.

5 **Jacksonville HD,** Southern Oregon Historical Society, Box 480, Jacksonville 97530. In 1852 when gold was struck at Rich Gulch, Jacksonville attracted hordes of gold seekers. For some 32 years the town prospered as a county seat and inland trade and financial center. Restored in the 1960's, Jacksonville again welcomes visitors to its 1880's heyday. Visitors pan for gold and examine 19th-century photographs, old banking equipment, period furnishings. The 1883 courthouse serves as a museum.

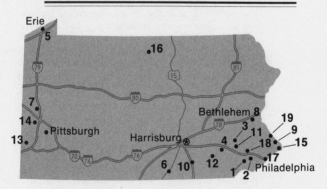

PENNSYLVANIA

1 **Brandywine Battlefield SHP,** U. S. 1, Chadds Ford 19317. George Washington's crushing defeat at the Battle of the Brandywine, September 11, 1777, left Philadelphia open to advancing British troops. Lafayette's quarters and the reconstructed headquarters of Washington highlight the 50-acre park. Also in the area are the John Chad House, where fighting took place; the Birmingham Friends Meeting House, used as a hospital after the battle; and the Brinton 1704 House, a stone Quaker dwelling.

2 **Colonial Pennsylvania Plantation,** Ridley Creek SP, Edgemont 19028. Specialists in history and folklore recreate daily activities on a typical working farm of the 1770's. See book, page 79.

3 **Daniel Boone Homestead,** Boone Rd., Birdsboro 19508. The famous trailblazer lived in a log cabin here from his birth in 1734 until 1750, when his Quaker family migrated to North Carolina. During the 18th century the present stone farmhouse, restored and furnished with period items, replaced the log structure. Nearby are a blacksmith shop, stone smokehouse, barn, restored log cabin, sawmill, and a museum of exhibits about Boone and rural life in 18th-century Pennsylvania.

4   **Ephrata Cloister,** 632 W. Main St., Ephrata 17522. Pre-Revolutionary War buildings survive in a medieval-style, German Protestant settlement where the oldest American-made press printed the largest book produced in colonial America. See book, page 223.

5   **Erie.** The Wayne Blockhouse, a replica of the one where "Mad Anthony" died in 1796 while fighting Indians, stands on the site of his original grave. The square-rigged *Niagara,* patterned after Commodore Perry's flagship in his 1813 victory over the British on Lake Erie, includes a sail bin, storerooms, and quarters for the captain and crew. The Perry Memorial House and Dickson Tavern, once a hostelry for Perry and other notables, is honeycombed with secret passages where runaway slaves hid before the Civil War. Modeled after the Roman Pantheon, the 1839 Old Custom House contains a museum highlighting the history of northwestern Pennsylvania. Write: Chamber of Commerce, 1006 State St., Erie 16501.

6   **Gettysburg NMP,** Gettysburg 17325. In the bloodiest battle of the Civil War, Gen. George Meade's Army of the Potomac defeated the Army of Northern Virginia under Gen. Robert E. Lee, July 1-3, 1863. See book, page 297.

7   **Harmony NHL,** Harmony 16037. The first village of the religious, communal Harmony Society includes the society's cemetery and the first Mennonite meeting house west of the Allegheny mountains. See book, page 224.

8   **Bethlehem HD,** 459 Old York Rd., Bethlehem 18018. Moravians from Central Europe settled here in 1741 as missionaries to the Indians. Living as a closed community for more than a century, the entire population resided at first in the five-story Gemein Haus. Now a museum, it displays early Moravian furniture, clocks, art, needlework, silver, and musical instruments. A springhouse, tannery, waterworks, miller's house, and the home of a prominent brewer recall Moravian days. Thick walls and massive buttresses distinguish the Old Chapel; the federal-style Central Moravian Church is noted for its belfry and hand-carved details. The Sun Inn hosted soldiers and statesmen during the Revolutionary War.

9   **Historic Fallsington, Inc.,** 4 Yardley Ave., Fallsington 19054. Visitors journey back to a town almost as unspoiled as when Quaker William Penn worshiped here some 300 years ago. Dwellings range from one of Pennsylvania's earliest log houses to Victorian extravaganzas. On Meetinghouse Square stand restored buildings, including an 18th-century inn. The 1789 Burges-Lippincott House boasts a beautiful doorway, carved fireplace, and a wing used as a doctor's office in the mid-1800's.

10   **Historical Society of York County Museum,** 250 E. Market St., York 17403. The Street of Shops and village square diorama capture the charm of colonial York. Rooms in the Bonham House range from a federal-style dining room to a Victorian parlor. To the rear of the half-timbered Golden Plough Tavern is General Gates' House, where Lafayette thwarted a conspiracy to overthrow Washington as commander of the Continental army. Pennsylvania Dutch furnishings decorate the 1812 Log House.

11   **Hopewell Village NHS,** Rte. 1, Box 345, Elverson 19520. A restored iron plantation, Hopewell produced stoves, castings, and pig iron from 1770 to 1883. See book, page 354.

12   **Lancaster.** In the heart of Pennsylvania Dutch country, the "plain people"—descendants of German, or *deutsch,* settlers—cling to their self-sufficient way of life. Tours of the Amish Homestead and the Amish Farm and House introduce visitors to early farming methods. At the

Pennsylvania Farm Museum of Landis Valley, more than 150,000 farm, household, and craft items illustrate the role of agriculture in the state's growth. The Railroad Museum of Pennsylvania depicts the history of rail transportation. James Buchanan, the only Pennsylvanian and bachelor President (1857-61), resided at Wheatland, a 17-room brick house. Write: Chamber of Commerce and Industry, 30 W. Orange St., Lancaster 17603.

13 Meadowcroft Village, Penowa Rd., Avella 15312. Restored 19th-century structures preserve the flavor of a pioneer farming community in western Pennsylvania. At the hub of this re-created village are a century-old covered bridge, log cabin, and one-room schoolhouse. Other buildings relocated in this wooded setting include a museum, barbershop, smokehouse, carriage barn, cobbler's shop, smithy, and well-stocked general stores.

14 Old Economy Village NHL, 14th and Church Sts., Ambridge 15003. Mass-produced houses, a vaulted wine cellar, and a Feast House capable of serving 800 diners highlight restoration of this prosperous Harmonist town at its zenith between 1830 and 1850. See book, page 227.

15 Pennsbury Manor, off Rte. 13, Morrisville 19067. William Penn's reconstructed manor, gardens, and outbuildings overlook the Delaware River. See book, page 30.

16 Pennsylvania Lumber Museum, Rte. 6, ten miles west of Galeton 16922. The story of 19th-century logging comes to life at two exhibit halls and a reconstructed lumber camp. Displays include a bunkhouse, enginehouse, steam locomotive, circular sawmill, and saw-filers' shack.

17 Philadelphia.
Fairmount Park. Restored country estates of wealthy Philadelphians grace this 8,900-acre park. William Penn's grandson built Solitude, and the patron of John James Audubon lived at Sweetbriar. Before being convicted of treason, Benedict Arnold bought Mount Pleasant as a wedding present for his bride. Ben Franklin often visited Woodford. Philadelphia-crafted Chippendale furniture highlights Cedar Grove; toys and gadgets fill the attic of Strawberry Mansion. Laurel Hill features a federal-style octagonal ballroom, and Lemon Hill boasts oval salons on three floors. Replicas of old trolleys circle the park and stop at buildings from the 1876 Centennial Exhibition.

Germantown HD. Dutch doors and arched cellar windows distinguish old homes in Germantown, settled by Hollanders in 1683 and a later contingent of Germans. In 1767 Benjamin Chew, attorney general and chief justice of colonial Pennsylvania, completed Cliveden. This Georgian home was badly damaged during the 1777 Battle of Germantown, when the stone walls of Grumblethorpe and Wyck echoed to cannon. Stenton, built in 1730 by William Penn's secretary, served as American and British headquarters during the Revolution. In 1793 and 1794 President and Mrs. Washington resided at the Deshler-Morris House, noted for its 24 large-paned windows.

Independence NHP. Many of early America's most significant events took place in old Philadelphia: meetings of the Continental Congress, adoption of the Declaration of Independence, ringing of the Liberty Bell, writing of the Constitution. Historical treasures include Independence Hall, Carpenters' Hall, Congress Hall, Bishop White House, Christ Church, Gloria Dei Church, City Tavern, Franklin Court. See book, page 165.

U.S.S. *Olympia*. Step aboard the 344-foot cruiser and relive the days when *Olympia* served as Commodore Dewey's flagship at the Battle of Manila Bay during the Spanish-American War. The oldest steel-hulled American warship still afloat bore the body of the Unknown Soldier from France after World War I. Visitors glimpse Dewey's quarters, the engine room, machine shop, galley, sick bay.

Society Hill HD. The oldest residential area in Philadelphia was named for William Penn's land development society. An 18th-century-style walled garden adjoins the

Samuel Powel House, where Washington, Lafayette, and other Revolutionary War heroes dined and danced. Period pieces decorate the Hill-Keith-Physick House, home of Dr. Philip Physick, "father of American surgery," and A Man Full of Trouble Tavern, which dates from 1759.

Write: Convention and Visitors Bureau, 3 Penn Center Plaza, Suite 2020, Philadelphia 19102.

18 **Valley Forge NHP,** Valley Forge 19481. General Washington's starving, tattered army bivouacked here from December 1777 to June 1778. Although 3,000 soldiers died that bitter winter, the survivors emerged as a rejuvenated army. Remains of fortifications and reconstructed soldiers' huts dot the 3,000-acre park. Also on view are Washington's Headquarters and the quarters of General Varnum. Nearby stand the Washington Memorial Chapel, a museum, and Mill Grove, first American home of naturalist John James Audubon. See book, page 137.

19 **Washington Crossing SP,** Washington Crossing 18977. In a blinding snowstorm on Christmas night 1776, George Washington and 2,400 soldiers assembled here and crossed the Delaware to attack Hessian mercenaries quartered in Trenton. The general and his officers laid plans for the attack at the Thompson-Neely House, a 1702 fieldstone farmhouse. Washington is believed to have eaten dinner that fateful evening at the Old Ferry Inn, restored as a museum. Sentries watched the river from Bowman's Hill, where an elevator whisks visitors to the top of an observation tower. The Memorial Building houses a Revolutionary-period museum.

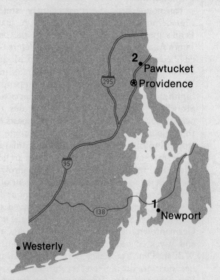

RHODE ISLAND

1 **Newport.** Restored architecture in Newport's waterfront area recalls its prosperous seaport days. Notable 18th-century buildings include Old Colony House NHL (1742), the state's first capitol; Hunter House NHL (1748), with furniture crafted by 18th-century Newport cabinetmakers; and Touro Synagogue NHL (1763), America's oldest synagogue. Newport is the site of the original U. S. Naval War College NHL, along with its modern successor. Lavish summer "cottages," built for Gilded Age millionaires at the turn of the century, welcome visitors. The Breakers, built for Cornelius Vanderbilt in 1895, contains original furnishings. Write: Newport County Chamber of Commerce, 10 America's Cup Ave., Newport 02840.

2 **Slater Mill NHS,** Box 727, Pawtucket 02862. This restored cotton mill commemorates the beginnings of America's cotton textile industry. See book, page 354.

SOUTH CAROLINA

1 | **Beaufort HD.** Chartered in 1711, this harbor town is the second oldest in the state. Spanish explorers visited the area in the 16th century; the French founded a short-lived colony here in 1562. Beaufort Museum, housed in a 1795 arsenal, displays relics of the town's long history. St. Helena's Episcopal Church, built in 1724, served as a hospital during the Civil War; tombstones were used as operating tables. Guided tours of the town are available; house tours are held each spring. Write: Chamber of Commerce, Box 910, Beaufort 29901. See book, page 120.

2 | **Camden.** Irish Quakers founded the first inland town in the state here in 1750. Revolutionary War battles raged in and around the town; most of it was burned by the British as they departed in 1781. The restored area features reconstructed remains of British forts. The three-story Cornwallis House was used as a headquarters by the British general. Write: Historic Camden, Camden 29020.

3 | **Charleston.** The long history of this coastal city extends back to its founding as an English colony in 1670. Write: Convention and Visitors' Bureau, Box 975, Charleston 29402. See book, page 114.

4 | **Cowpens NB.** Located 11 miles northwest of I-85 at Gaffney, this small preserve commemorates a key Revolutionary War battle. On January 17, 1781, patriots under command of Brig. Gen. Daniel Morgan met a superior British force led by Lt. Col. Banastre Tarleton. Morgan turned a retreat into victory by rallying his troops to stand and fire. Write: Superintendent, Cowpens NB, Box 308, Chesnee 29323.

5 | **Fort Sumter NM,** 1214 Middle St., Sullivans Island 29482. The Civil War's first engagement took place at this site. See book, pages 263, 289.

6 | **Georgetown HD.** Third oldest town in the state, Georgetown was founded in 1729 as a shipping center for rice and indigo planters. At the Rice Museum, exhibits recount the development of rice planting in the United States. Historic buildings include Prince George Winyah Church, built in 1737 with brick brought from England. The Kaminski House, a typical low-country mansion, is furnished with antiques dating from the 15th century. Write: Chamber of Commerce, Box 1776, Georgetown 29442.

7 | **Kings Mountain NMP.** Remote settlements west of the Alleghenies were little affected by the Revolutionary War until 1780, when the British, halted in the North, began a conquest of the South. Then the mountain men formed regiments and harassed the redcoats with guerrilla warfare, culminating on October 7 in a vicious battle at this site near the state's northern border. Exhibits, monuments, and markers throughout the park's 4,000 acres describe the battle, decisively won by the patriots; a foot trail wanders the battlefield ridge. Write: Superintendent, Box 31, Kings Mountain, North Carolina 28086.

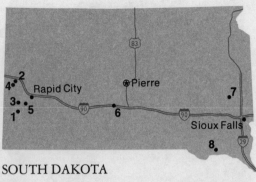

SOUTH DAKOTA

1 | **Custer SP**, U. S. 16, Custer 57730. Within this 73,000-acre park stands a replica of the historic Gordon Stockade, built by the gold-seeking Gordon party in the winter of 1874-75. Lured by tales of strikes in the Black Hills, these prospectors squatted illegally on Indian land, built crude cabins beside French Creek, fenced them in with a stockade, and panned for gold until the U. S. Cavalry moved them out of the territory. One of the nation's largest buffalo herds roams the park. Natural history exhibits are on display.

2 | **Deadwood HD**, 735 Main St., Deadwood 57732. After gold was discovered in the Black Hills in 1874, Deadwood boomed. Today its main street, set in a gulch and lined with several original buildings, evokes the untamed spirit of its mining days. The remains of "Wild Bill" Hickok—shot in the back by Jack McCall during a poker game in 1876—"Calamity Jane" Cannary, Deadwood Dick, and other locals who made frontier history lie in Boot Hill Cemetery on nearby Mount Moriah. Centennial Theater re-enacts colorful dramas from Deadwood's past. The Adams Memorial Museum contains pioneer exhibits. Visitors tour the Broken Boot Gold Mine to view early mining processes and equipment.

3 | **1880 Train**, Box 1880, Hill City 57745. Vintage steam locomotives haul open and closed coaches daily on a 1¾-hour round trip between the old mining camps of Hill City and Keystone Junction. The scenic ride follows the historical "prospectors' route," passing the sites of several 19th-century mines. At one point the train climbs the nation's steepest regular railroad grade.

4 | **Homestake Mine**, Main St., Lead 57754. Visitors tour the surface operations of the largest gold mine in the United States. The mine, more than a mile deep in places, has been worked continuously since 1876, except for a short period during World War II.

5 | **Keystone.** Massive, 60- to 70-foot-high heads of George Washington, Thomas Jefferson, Theodore Roosevelt, and Abraham Lincoln took shape on the granite face of Mount Rushmore NMem under the direction of sculptor Gutzon Borglum between 1927 and 1941. During summer, amphitheater programs dramatize details of the project and the philosophies of these four Presidents. Big Thunder Gold Mine offers tours and interprets local geology and history. At the end of the tour, visitors are given hammers and chisels and an opportunity to mine a sample from deep in the mine. Write: Convention-Visitors Bureau, Box 747, Rapid City 57709.

6 | **Pioneer Auto Museum and Antique Town**, Box 76, Murdo 57559. This ten-acre site contains authentic turn-of-the century buildings and more than 250 antique and classic cars, including a 1902 Oldsmobile, 1909 Sears-Roebuck, 1925 Stanley Steamer, and Fords from 1906 to 1932. A livery barn houses a collection of sleighs, buggies, surreys, and other horse-drawn vehicles. Early bicycles and motorcycles, farm tractors, antique American furnishings, and music boxes also are displayed. Among the old-time buildings are a 1906 jail, a homesteader's claim cabin, one-room schoolhouse, barber and black-smith shops, and a general store.

7 **Prairie Village,** Rte. 34, Madison 57042. Some 50 buildings, most moved to this 140-acre site from towns throughout the state, re-create a typical pioneer village. Attractions include an 1877 claim shanty, a sod house, an 1872 two-story hand-hewn log dwelling, an 1884 one-room schoolhouse, the first chartered library in the Dakota Territory, and a 1912 opera house which presents repertory theater productions during the summer. Also on display are antique tractors and working steam-powered machines, including an 1893 carousel and a German loco-motive. Write: Prairie Historical Society, Box 256, Madison 57042.

8 **Yankton.** Nineteenth-century houses still line the flower-trimmed streets of the earliest settlement and first capital of the Dakota Territory, the town where Jack McCall was hanged for the murder of "Wild Bill" Hickok. A museum in Westside Park recalls territorial days through period rooms, historic artifacts, and exhibits. Among its attractions: a replica of the first territorial governor's office, an Indian tepee, sodbuster plow, wooden sleigh, and schoolroom. Write: Chamber of Commerce, 104 E. Fourth St., Yankton 57078.

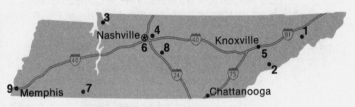

TENNESSEE

1 **Andrew Johnson NHS,** Depot St., Greeneville 37743. Three areas make up this memorial to the 17th President (1865-69) and the only one to be tried under impeachment proceedings. The Andrew Johnson Homestead was his home from 1851 until his death in 1875; most of its furnishings are original. Johnson is buried in Monument Hill Cemetery. His first trade, tailoring, is recalled in the shop which houses Johnson's old tailor's bench, stove, shears, and other implements.

2 **Cades Cove,** Great Smoky Mountains NP, off Little River Rd., near Gatlinburg 37738. The log cabins, churches, mills, and farms built by pioneers in this valley during the early 1800's have been restored as an open-air museum. Visitors wend an 11-mile drive past homesteads and open fields. A short foot trail leads to the John Oliver cabin, home of the valley's first white settler.

Chickamauga and Chattanooga NMP. See Georgia.

3 **Fort Donelson NMP,** Dover 37058. The Union army saw its first major victory of the Civil War here in 1862 when Gen. Simon Buckner surrendered 13,000 Confederate soldiers to Gen. Ulysses S. Grant after a four-day battle—the largest number of men ever to surrender at one time in North America. The victory boosted Union morale and brought Grant's military abilities to light. The earthworks of the fort, Confederate river batteries, more than two miles of trenches, and a reconstructed powder magazine are preserved. A slide show and museum highlight the battle.

4 **Historic Hermitage Properties,** 4580 Rachel's Lane, Hermitage 37076. The 625-acre estate near Nashville was for 40 years the home of Andrew Jackson, 7th President (1829-37). The Hermitage, built in 1819, is a relatively simple structure, but retains the columns of the Greek Revival style of its day. It is furnished with Jackson's possessions, including "Old Hickory's" favorite armchair. The red brick Old Hermitage Church stands on the estate; Mrs. Jackson was very religious and, to please her, Jackson contributed heavily to its building fund. Nearby Tulip Grove, a colonnaded antebellum house, was the home of Mrs. Jackson's nephew.

5   **Knoxville.** Founded after the Revolutionary War as a repair and supply center for westbound wagon trains, Knoxville was badly damaged during the Civil War. Several homes from the early years have been restored. Gen. James White's Fort, built by the area's first settler, includes the main house and three log cabins for visitors, enclosed by a stockade against Indian attacks.

Marble Springs Historic Farm NHL, built as a trading post and refuge for settlers by Tennessee's first governor, John Sevier, features a two-story log house, along with a barn, loom house, kitchen, and smokehouse.

Blount Mansion NHL, one of the oldest frame houses west of the Allegheny Mountains, was built in 1792 for William Blount, who was appointed by George Washington as governor of the territory south of the Ohio River. Its 18th-century furnishings include an extensive collection of pewter kitchenware.

The stately Ramsey House NHS, constructed in 1797 of local pink marble and limestone, displays antique quilts, costumes, tools, and utensils; 18th-century home crafts are demonstrated. Bleak House, a 15-room antebellum mansion used as a headquarters by Confederate Gen. James Longstreet, is a museum of Southern history. Write: Visitors Bureau, Box 15012, Knoxville 37901.

6   **Nashville.** Fort Nashborough is a reconstruction of the 1779 pioneer fort from which the city of Nashville grew. The Travellers' Rest Historic House was built in 1799 by John Overton, a law partner of Andrew Jackson and a founder of Memphis. The 16-room dwelling, now a historic museum, contains colonial- and federal-style furniture. The Greek Revival mansion Belle Meade, built in 1853, is filled with 19th-century furnishings. Its outbuildings include an 1890's carriage house and a stone dairy house of Tudor-Gothic style.

Nearby, two churches, both completed in the early 1850's, survived the devastation of the Civil War. The Downtown Presbyterian Church was used from 1862-65 as a Union hospital; cavalry horses were stabled in the basement. The exterior of this Egyptian Revival structure remains almost unchanged since that time. The Holy Trinity Episcopal Church housed Union supplies and gunpowder. Cleaver marks may still be seen on the altar, used by troops as a butcher block. Write: Chamber of Commerce, 161 Fourth Ave. N., Nashville 37219.

7   **Shiloh NMP,** Hwy. 22, Shiloh 38376. The first major western engagement of the Civil War took place here on April 6-7, 1862. The Union victory led to eventual control of the Mississippi River. Visitors to Shiloh take a self-guiding auto tour of the battlefield. See book, page 297.

8   **Stones River NB,** Rte. 10, Box 401, Old Nashville Hwy., Murfreesboro 37130. The three-day battle that began here on December 31, 1862, claimed 23,000 casualties but gained no military advantage for either side. Confederate troops withdrew; Union forces camped at Murfreesboro for six months before resuming the offensive. A slide program and exhibits explain the battle; an auto tour includes the Union cemetery and the oldest Civil War memorial.

9   **Victorian Village, Inc. HD,** 4140 Chanwill Ave., Memphis 38117. Nine of the city's oldest residences stand in this historic district. The Fontaine House, a brick home with furniture ranging from colonial to late Victorian, includes a children's dollhouse, a neighboring carriage house, and gingerbread playhouse. The Mallory-Neely House, Victorian to its towers, turrets, and stained-glass windows, contains original family furnishings.

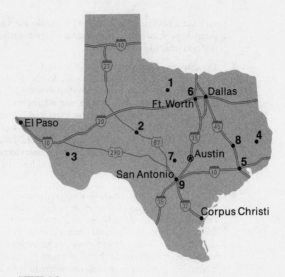

TEXAS

1 | **Fort Belknap,** Hwy. 380, Newcastle 76372. This 1851 fort, built to protect settlers from marauding Indians, has been restored to show early Texas life. The commissary, powder magazine, cornhouse, and three infantry barracks have been reconstructed. Two museums display relics of frontier days and a collection of ladies' apparel.

2 | **Fort Concho Preservation and Museum,** 213 E. Ave. D, San Angelo 76903. Best preserved fort of the Indian wars in Texas and headquarters of the 10th Cavalry—a black regiment known as the "Buffalo Soldiers"—Fort Concho maintains 16 original buildings and 4 reconstructed ones. The 1876 administration building and two rebuilt barracks now serve as a museum. Displays include pioneer relics and guns.

3 | **Fort Davis NHS,** Fort Davis 79734. Troops stationed here protected travelers on the Overland Trail from 1854 to 1891. Founded by Jefferson Davis, then Secretary of War, the fort played a major role in the defense of western Texas. Of the more than 60 buildings that once stood here, 24 are preserved today, including officers' quarters, troop barracks, and the post commissary. Military and Indian exhibits are housed in these buildings, as well as audio-visual programs.

4 | **Heritage Garden Village and Museum,** Woodville 75979. Thirty original buildings form this pioneer village, including an 1866 log cabin, post office, blacksmith shop, apothecary, and other businesses, all furnished and equipped as they were in the late 19th century. Visitors sample the past by using an old-time wall telephone, a butter churn, and an early sewing machine.

5 | **Houston.** Named for Sam Houston, a hero of the war for Texas independence, this city began as a riverboat landing in 1836. The Harris County Heritage Society Buildings in Sam Houston Park have been restored and furnished to re-create 19th-century life. San Jacinto SHP, a 460-acre park located 21 miles east of the city on the Houston Ship Channel, commemorates the struggle against Mexican domination. Here was fought the final battle that won independence for Texas—until its annexation by the United States in 1845. A 570-foot-high monument housing a museum of Texas history marks the site. Also at the park is the U.S.S. *Texas,* a battleship which saw action in both World Wars and served as the flagship off Normandy on D-Day. Write: Chamber of Commerce, 3300 Main St., Houston 77002.

6 | **Log Cabin Village,** Log Cabin Village Lane, Fort Worth 76109. Because details are known about the original owners of these seven log and mud cabins, visitors can envision real pioneer families living here. Period furnishings, tools, and household equipment help make the visit a personal one. Costumed guides demonstrate such frontier crafts as quilting and weaving.

7 **Lyndon B. Johnson NHP,** Johnson City 78636. The site consists of two separate areas. In the Johnson City unit, the boyhood home of the 36th President (1963-69) has been restored to its appearance during the 1922-25 period. The Johnson Settlement, restored homestead of LBJ's grandfather, stands half a mile away and can be reached by a self-guided walking trail. The LBJ Ranch, 15 miles west on U. S. 290, includes the reconstructed farmhouse where Johnson was born in 1908, his first school, his ranch, and grave site.

8 **Sam Houston Memorial,** Box 2057, Huntsville 77341. Sam Houston, hero of the Battle of San Jacinto, became the first president of the Lone Star Republic and first senator from the newly admitted state of Texas. The home he designed and built in 1847 served as his residence for 11 years. He then moved to the "Steamboat House," built to resemble a Mississippi steamboat, where he died in 1863. Also here are his law office and the Sam Houston Memorial Museum, which contains personal belongings and relics from the Texas revolutionary period.

9 **San Antonio.** First a Spanish, then a Mexican outpost until the 1835-36 Texan revolution, this city retains much of its colorful heritage. Restored Spanish missions include the 1720 Mission San José, which embraces a church, convent, granary, Indian quarters, and an old mill; Mission San Francisco de la Espada and Mission San Juan Capistrano, both established in 1731. La Villita is an authentic restoration of San Antonio's earliest community. The Spanish Governor's Palace housed rulers of the Spanish province of Texas for almost 100 years. The Alamo commemorates the 187 Texans, including Jim Bowie, Davy Crockett, and William Travis, who died here in 1836 resisting a 13-day siege by General Santa Anna's troops. Write: Convention and Visitors Bureau, Box 2277, San Antonio 78298. See book, page 204.

UTAH

1 **Camp Floyd SHS,** Fairfield 84013. Established in 1858 and abandoned three years later, Camp Floyd was the largest U. S. Army encampment of its time, with a garrison of 4,000 men. Federal troops stationed here had been sent to quell a Mormon "rebellion" and stayed as a local law enforcement agency. The Stagecoach Inn and the old army commissary have been restored. The inn served as a Pony Express stop and a station for the Overland Stage. The Johnston Army Cemetery holds the graves of 84 soldiers who died at the camp.

2   **Golden Spike NHS**, Box W, Brigham City 84302. This site commemorates the completion of the first American transcontinental railroad. Re-enactments of the Last Spike Ceremony take place on May 10 and the second Saturday in August. See book, page 322.

3   **Salt Lake City.** Founded in 1847 by Brigham Young, the city remains world headquarters for the Church of Jesus Christ of Latter-day Saints. Within the walled Temple Square stand the monumental granite Mormon Temple (not open to the public) and the oval-domed Mormon Tabernacle, where the great pipe organ and choir may be heard. The Beehive House, built in 1854 as Young's official residence, and his grave are also on view. Other points of interest include the Pioneer Trail SP and the magnificent State Capitol, with a panoramic view of the city. Write: Salt Lake Area Chamber of Commerce, 175 E. 400 South, Salt Lake City 84111. See book, page 255.

VERMONT

1   **Bennington.** Bennington Museum displays Early American memorabilia and a collection of Grandma Moses paintings. It also operates the restored 18th-century Peter Matteson Tavern in neighboring Shaftsbury. The Old First Church, restored to its early 19th-century appearance, contains in its cemetery the graves of poet Robert Frost and soldiers who died in the 1777 Battle of Bennington. Write: Chamber of Commerce, Veterans Memorial Dr., Bennington 05201.

2   **Calvin Coolidge Homestead NHL**, Plymouth Notch 05056. In the early morning of August 3, 1923, Vice President Calvin Coolidge was sworn in as 30th President (1923-29) in this simple white frame farmhouse. News of President Warren G. Harding's death had just reached him during a visit to his boyhood home. Coolidge's father, a notary public, administered the oath. The house has been restored with many of the original furnishings. Coolidge's birthplace across the street has also been restored.

3   **Shelburne Museum**, Shelburne 05482. This 45-acre outdoor museum records three centuries of American life. The collection includes 18th- and 19th-century homes, stores, a jail, stagecoach inn, railroad station with locomotive and private car, and a lighthouse. Most unusual exhibit is the 1906 side-wheeler S.S. *Ticonderoga* NHL, the last passenger steamer to ply Lake Champlain. A varied collection of Americana ranges from paintings and pewter to coaches, snuffboxes, and toys.

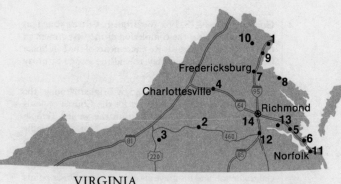

VIRGINIA

1 | **Alexandria.** Sections of this port city retain their 18th-century appearance. Write: Tourist Council, 221 King St., Alexandria 22314. See book, page 178.

2 | **Appomattox Court House NHP,** Box 218, Appomattox 24522. On Palm Sunday, April 9, 1865, Confederate Gen. Robert E. Lee surrendered to Union Gen. Ulysses S. Grant at the Wilmer McLean House, a gracious brick dwelling in the village of Appomattox Court House. McLean House and the courthouse have been reconstructed. Clover Hill Tavern, Meeks General Store, and other buildings have been restored. A self-guiding history trail takes visitors to the Confederate cemetery and the site of Lee's headquarters. See book, page 302.

1 | **Arlington House, The Robert E. Lee Memorial.** This antebellum mansion, situated on a hilltop overlooking Washington, D. C., was the Custis family home from 1802 and the scene of Mary Custis's wedding to Robert E. Lee in 1831. The Lees lived here until the Civil War, when federal forces seized the house. See book, page 270.

In 1864 Arlington National Cemetery was established on the property. Among the graves are those of Robert E. Peary, Oliver Wendell Holmes, William Howard Taft, and thousands of war veterans. Visitors may board tourmobiles that stop at Arlington House, the Tomb of the Unknowns, and the graves of John F. Kennedy and Robert F. Kennedy. Write: Arlington National Cemetery, Arlington 22211. See book, page 388.

3 | **Booker T. Washington NM,** Rte. 1, Box 195, Hardy 24101. The Burroughs Plantation—a small tobacco farm—was the birthplace in 1856 of a slave who rose to become a distinguished educator and national leader. The plantation includes a replica of the log cabin described by Washington as his childhood home. Corn and tobacco grow in the fields; pastures and pens hold cows, sheep, chickens, pigs. Exhibits and an audiovisual program describe Washington's career.

4 | **Charlottesville HD.** Thomas Jefferson founded and designed the University of Virginia here in 1819. Numerous other restored buildings and homes in the town reflect his architectural influence. Nearby is James Monroe's country estate, Ash Lawn, and Jefferson's own beloved mansion, Monticello (see below). Write: Visitors Bureau, Box 161, Charlottesville 22902. See book, page 188.

5 | **Colonial NHP,** Yorktown 23690. A 23-mile parkway connects Jamestown, the first permanent English settlement; Yorktown, site of the last major battle of the American Revolution; and Williamsburg, colonial capital of Virginia. See book, pages 32, 83, 140.

6 | **Fort Monroe,** Casemate Museum, Box 341, Fort Monroe 23651. Two earlier forts occupied Old Point Comfort near Hampton before moat-encircled Fort Monroe was erected in 1819. Robert E. Lee helped supervise construction of the fort; Edgar Allan Poe served here and Abraham Lincoln slept here. This "Gibraltar of the Chesapeake" remained a Union stronghold during the Civil War. Confederacy President Jefferson Davis was imprisoned here for two years. His cell is now part of the Casemate Museum, located in the fort's walls. Scale models depict the battle between the ironclad ships *Merrimack* and *Monitor,* which clashed in battle within sight of the fort on March 9, 1862.

7 **Fredericksburg.** Reminders of our first President fill this town, founded in 1727. Though badly damaged in the Civil War, many historic buildings have been restored. Self-guided walking or driving tours include Mary Washington House, bought by Washington in 1772 for his mother; Rising Sun Tavern, built in 1760 by Washington's brother Charles; the Georgian mansion Kenmore, home of Washington's sister, Betty; and Mercer Apothecary, where Washington had an office. Mementos of another President, James Monroe, may be seen in the building that served as his first law office. Write: Visitor Center, 706 Caroline St., Fredericksburg 22401.

Fredericksburg and Spotsylvania NMP in and around the town includes four major Civil War battlefields and the house where Stonewall Jackson died after the Battle of Chancellorsville. Visitors follow conducted or self-guiding tours. Write: Superintendent, Box 679, Fredericksburg 22404. See book, page 294.

8 **George Washington Birthplace NM,** Rte. 1, Box 717, Washington's Birthplace 22575. This site is a re-creation of 18th-century Popes Creek Plantation. See book, page 168.

9 **Gunston Hall Plantation,** Lorton 22079. This mansion overlooking the Potomac River was the home of George Mason. See book, page 111.

10 **Manassas NBP,** Box 1830, Manassas 22110. Two major Civil War battles scarred these rolling Virginia hills near Bull Run and the Manassas railroad center. At First Manassas in 1861, where Union forces were routed by Confederate troops, Gen. Thomas J. Jackson won the nickname "Stonewall." At Second Manassas a year later, Confederate armies were again victorious, and Gen. Robert E. Lee began to move into the North. Exhibits and programs describe the campaigns; trails and roads take visitors to battle sites, a cemetery, monuments, and original buildings, including restored Stone House, a tavern used by the Union as a field hospital. See book, page 290.

4 **Monticello.** Located near Charlottesville, this imposing mansion was designed by Jefferson and served as his home from 1769 to 1826. Write: Thomas Jefferson Memorial Foundation, Monticello 22902. See book, page 182.

9 **Mount Vernon.** George Washington lived on this Potomac River estate. Write: Mount Vernon Ladies' Association, Mount Vernon 22121. See book, page 168.

11 **Norfolk.** One of the nation's oldest brick houses, Adam Thoroughgood House, defied the wilderness here in 1650. Today, restored and refurnished, it graces the largest city in Virginia. First settled in 1682, Norfolk was a thriving seaport by 1728. In 1776 departing Royal Governor Lord Dunmore burned the town. One souvenir remains—a cannonball embedded in a wall of St. Paul's Church. A new town quickly rose at the deep harbor, now home of the world's largest naval base. Self-guiding tours include the restored Willoughby-Baylor and Myers houses, elegant federal-style town houses built before 1800. Daytime and evening harbor cruises (except in winter) pass ships, submarines, and shipyards. Write: Convention and Visitors Bureau, 208 E. Plume St., Norfolk 23501.

12 **Petersburg NB,** Box 549, Petersburg 23804. In June 1864, Union forces, unable to break the Confederate line at Petersburg, began a siege. For ten months, Confederate forces held the city as Union troops cut supply lines. Some 70,000 lives were lost before the siege ended April 2, 1865, with Lee's withdrawal. A few weeks later the war ended at Appomattox. Fortifications and ruins remain along a tour road to The Crater, scene of a spectacular failure. The Union used the skills of Pennsylvania coal miners to tunnel underground and blast a huge gap in the Confederate line, then blundered in following up their advantage, losing the area to the Confederates.

13 **Plantations of the Tidewater-James River area.** Write: Virginia Division of Tourism, 202 North Ninth St., Richmond 23219. See book, page 102.

14 **Richmond HD.** In 1737 William Byrd II drew plans for a city at a trading-post site near the James River Falls. In 1779 Richmond became the capital of Virginia and in 1861 the capital of the Confederacy. Much of the city burned during the Civil War, but many historic buildings and houses remain, including the capitol, designed by Thomas Jefferson and built in 1788, and St. John's Episcopal Church, scene of Patrick Henry's "give me liberty or give me death" speech. The Confederate White House (1817) now serves as a Civil War museum. Write: Visitors Center, 1700 Robin Hood Rd., Richmond 23220.

Richmond NBP preserves nine Civil War battle sites in and around the city. Write: Superintendent, 3215 E. Broad St., Richmond 23223.

5 **Williamsburg.** The restored colonial capital includes more than a hundred buildings. Carter's Grove Plantation is nearby. Write: Colonial Williamsburg Foundation, Box C, Williamsburg 23187. See book, page 83.

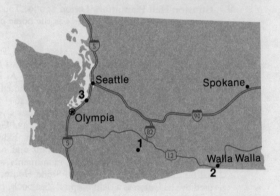

WASHINGTON

1 **Fort Simcoe SHP**, Rte. 1, Box 39, White Swan 98952. This 200-acre park contains one of the two U. S. Army posts established in the Washington Territory after a flare-up of Indian hostilities about 1856. Advance post for an infantry regiment until 1859, Fort Simcoe later served as an Indian agency and school on the Yakima Indian Reservation. The commandant's house, three captains' dwellings, two blockhouses, and the barracks have been restored and furnished.

2 **Fort Walla Walla Museum**, Box 1616, Walla Walla 99362. The U. S. Army built this post in 1856 for protection against hostile Indians. The past lives on in original and rebuilt structures—an early homestead, schoolhouse, cabin, country store, and blacksmith shop. Also on display is the West's largest collection of horse-drawn farm equipment.

Klondike Gold Rush NHP, Seattle. See Alaska.

3 **Point Defiance Park**, Tacoma. The 700-acre city park contains partly restored Fort Nisqually, moved here from its original location. The park includes the fort's granary, the oldest building in Washington. Camp Six, a replica steam logging camp of turn-of-the-century vintage, includes donkey engines, old tracks and trestles, railroad-car camps, and an operating steam locomotive. The 1865 Job Carr House, believed to be the first home in Old Tacoma, also stands in the park. Write: Fort Nisqually, Tacoma 98407.

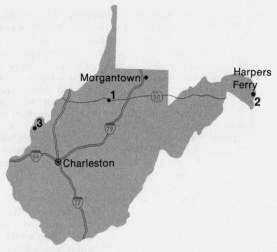

WEST VIRGINIA

1 | **Fort New Salem**, Salem 26426. After divided loyalties during the Revolution split the Seventh Day Baptist Church of Salem, New Jersey, 72 members of the congregation departed in 1792 to make a new home in the wilderness. Their settlement has been reconstructed by Salem College. Fifteen original log buildings serve as living museums, craft workshops, and college classrooms for the study of frontier life.

2 | **Harpers Ferry NHP**, Box 65, Harpers Ferry 25425. This restored 19th-century town was the scene of abolitionist John Brown's raid on a federal arsenal. The courthouse in nearby Charles Town incorporates the original 1801 building where John Brown was tried. See book, page 264.

3 | **Point Pleasant Battle Monument**, Tu-Endie-Wei Park, Point Pleasant 25550. Here on October 10, 1774, at the confluence of the Great Kanawha and Ohio Rivers, Virginia frontiersmen defeated Shawnees in the final battle of Lord Dunmore's War, a campaign to subdue the Indians. Nearby stands the log Mansion House, built as a tavern in 1796. Now restored, its antique furnishings include one of the first pianos brought over the Alleghenies.

WISCONSIN

1 | **Green Bay.** The oldest permanent settlement in the state, Green Bay was claimed for France by explorer Jean Nicolet in 1634. Historical structures from throughout the area have been relocated at Heritage Hill SP. The Roi-Porlier-Tank Cottage, oldest standing house in Wisconsin, was erected in 1776 by fur trader Joseph Roi and served as a

British headquarters during the War of 1812. The Fort Howard complex was constructed soon after that war. The Cotton House, considered one of the finest examples of Jeffersonian architecture in the Midwest, was built in 1840 by Capt. John W. Cotton. The Baird Law Office (1840) was originally built as a territorial land office. Other buildings in the park include the Franklin Fire House, a fur trader's cabin, a sugar camp, post office, general store, blacksmith shop, town hall, and a Norwegian barn.

Hazelwood, a frame house with dormer windows and colonnaded porches, was built in 1837 by Morgan L. Martin, a pioneer lawyer and legislator. Richly furnished with antiques, this riverfront house reflects the life of the prosperous resident of frontier Green Bay.

The National Railroad Museum displays a collection of historic locomotives and cars that evoke the romance of railroading days. President Eisenhower's locomotive, command car, and staff car from World War II; a Pullman parlor car used by Sir Winston Churchill; and the largest steam engine ever built are among the hundreds of railroad relics housed in this replica of an old depot. Visitors ride a 1910 standard-gauge steam train, and a special, narrow-gauge train takes children on rides. Write: Chamber of Commerce, Box 969, Green Bay 54305.

2 **Historic Galloway House and Village,** 336 Old Pioneer Rd., Fond du Lac 54935. A restored 30-room Victorian mansion with carved woodwork, stenciled ceiling, and many original furnishings serves as focal point of this complex. On its grounds stand a carriage house, gazebo, gardens, and a re-created pioneer village of the late 1800's. Among the 19th-century buildings are an original log house, working printshop, operating gristmill, one-room school, country store, dress shop, and veterinary clinic. Exhibits include farm equipment and vehicles, tools, clothing, household items, and toys of the period.

3 **Historylands Logging Camp,** County Road B, Hayward 54843. The reconstructed logging camp features lumbering operations of the past, a log bunkhouse, and a cook shanty housing a museum. A paddle-wheel steamboat, the *Namekagon Queen,* takes visitors on hourly river excursions. Lumberjack World Championships are held here in July. Competitions preserve such old skills as sawing, chopping, speed climbing, and log-rolling, or "birling."

4 **Little Norway,** near U. S. 18-151, Blue Mounds 53517. This 1856 farmstead contains the log house, barns, and outbuildings erected by one of the first Norwegian families to settle in the area. A replica of a 12th-century stave church, its gables adorned with dragons to ward off evil spirits, houses an exhibit of Norwegian antiques—handcarved skis, chests, rocking chairs, cupboards, embroidered hangings, jewelry, and an original manuscript by composer Edvard Grieg.

5 **Old Wade House SP,** Rte. 23, Greenbush 53026. The Wade House, a white-pillared stagecoach inn built in 1850, served settlers traveling the old plank road between Sheboygan and Fond du Lac. Included within the 270-acre grounds are a smokehouse, blacksmith shop, and Robinson House, a 19th-century residence. A one-mile ride along gravel paths in a horse-drawn carriage takes visitors to the Jung Carriage Museum, which shelters about 100 antique coaches, wagons, and sleighs.

6 **Paul Bunyan Logging Camp;** Chippewa Valley Museum, Carson Park, Eau Claire 54701. This replica of a 40-man lumber camp of the late 1890's was erected in the 1920's as a memorial to Wisconsin's pioneer lumberjacks. It includes a bunkhouse, cook's shanty, blacksmith's shop, stables, and sheds. The museum contains 76 major exhibits, from the Woodland Indians through the exploring, trapping, logging, farming, and industrial growth periods; also Sunnyview School, a typical one-room frontier schoolhouse built in 1880, and the Lars Anderson log cabin dating from 1960. Visitors can also find in Carson Park nature trails and a miniature railroad.

7   **Pendarvis HS,** 114 Shake Rag St., Mineral Point 53565. Several restored stone and log houses and a "kiddlywink" (pub), built by Cornish miners in the 1840's, recall the days when southwest Wisconsin was tough lead miners' land. Skilled in stonecutting and masonry, these Cornish "Jacks" constructed the first permanent houses in the area, limestone dwellings much like the ones they left in England. The Wisconsin Historical Society has furnished the houses with antiques and mining artifacts.

8   **Stonefield,** Nelson Dewey SP, Cassville 53806. On this 2,000-acre farm, once run like a Virginia plantation by Nelson Dewey, Wisconsin's first governor, stands a 19th-century frontier village. Twenty-five buildings, including a general store, a one-room schoolhouse, a pharmacy stocked with cure-alls, a printshop, firehouse, and bank, recall life at the turn of the century. Across a covered bridge, the restored Dewey homestead depicts the life of this gentleman-farmer; a nearby museum recalls the small farmers' more arduous days through exhibits of early farm tools and machines and shops of pre-industrial craftsmen. Horse-drawn carriages shuttle visitors around the grounds.

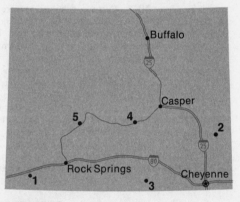

WYOMING

1   **Fort Bridger SHS,** U. S. 30S, Fort Bridger 82933. Established as a trading post in 1843 by mountain man Jim Bridger, the fort grew into a major army post along the northern route between the Missouri River and Pacific coast. Now partially restored, the fort includes a guardhouse, two officers' quarters, commissary, a replica of Bridger's trading post, Pony Express stables, and a museum with military, pioneer, and Indian relics and exhibits of Wyoming's fur-trapping days. Living history interpretive demonstrations are given during the summer.

2   **Fort Laramie NHS,** Rte. 26, Fort Laramie 82212. Originally founded as a fur-trading center in 1834, this fort was taken over by the army to safeguard travelers on the Oregon Trail. See book, page 250.

3   **Grand Encampment Museum,** Encampment 82325. Several historic buildings, including a log cabin, ranch house, stagecoach station, saloon, and printshop, have been moved to this site to re-create part of a pioneer mining town. Relics of the area's copper-mining boom, which lasted from about 1897 to 1908, are on display and include early horse-drawn vehicles, old mining equipment and wearing apparel, stock certificates of overpromoted copper mines, and other memorabilia of this small town's big days.

4   **Independence Rock NHL,** Rte. 220, 45 miles southwest of Casper 82601. Known as "the great registry of the desert," the 193-foot rock promontory, a natural landmark and popular camping site on the Oregon Trail, bears the messages and inscriptions of numerous westward-bound pioneers. See book, page 255.

5 | **South Pass City SHS,** off Rte. 28, 33 miles south of Lander 82520. A boomtown of the gold mining era, South Pass City won distinction as the initiator, in Wyoming's territorial legislature, of the 1869 bill that granted women equal suffrage for the first time in the United States. After the Carissa Lode's gold was depleted in the 1870's, the place became a ghost town. Today South Pass City is undergoing restoration. Untouched and restored buildings now stand side by side, and a museum recalls the locale's picturesque past. Nearby rises South Pass NHL, the 7,550-foot-high break in the Rockies through which traders and pioneers crossed the Continental Divide.

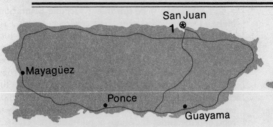

PUERTO RICO

1 | **San Juan NHS.** Massive 16th- and 17th-century fortifications built by the Spanish protected the colonial city and the treasure-laden ships that passed its way. Major attractions include thick-walled Castillo El Morro, rising 140 feet out of the sea to guard the harbor entrance; Castillo San Cristóbal, a cluster of five fortresses at the eastern edge of Old San Juan, with gun rooms and barracks surrounding its courtyard; and San Juan Gate, a remaining portion of the old city wall. The governor's palace, La Fortaleza, erected as a fortress in the 1530's, remains the oldest executive mansion in the Western Hemisphere still in use. Write: Institute of Puerto-Rican Culture, Old San Juan 00902. See book, page 21.

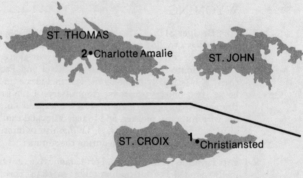

VIRGIN ISLANDS

1 | **Christiansted NHS,** Box 160, Christiansted, St. Croix 00820. Discovered by Columbus in 1493 and center of a rich Danish sugar empire in the 18th and early 19th centuries, St. Croix was purchased by the United States in 1917. In historic Christiansted, remnants of the old Danish way of life linger. A walking tour takes visitors to Fort Christiansvaern, Old Danish Customs House, scale house, Government House (capitol of the Danish West Indies), the Danish West India & Guinea Company Warehouse, and the Steeple Building, now a museum containing exhibits of pre-Columbian Indian history.

2 | **St. Thomas.** Fort Christian, completed by the Danes in the 1680's, stands as the oldest structure in the Virgin Islands. The St. Thomas Museum traces the island's colorful history. Write: Virgin Islands NP, Box 7789, Charlotte Amalie, St. Thomas 00801.